Split the Baby:

One Child's Journey

through Medicine and Law

Mary Ellen Mannix

Early praise for "Split the Baby: A Child's Journey
Through Medicine and Law":

"Mary Ellen Mannix has written a poignant and introspective book about how 21st century U.S. health care can cause more harm than good. It is a wake-up call for all mothers and fathers, sisters and brothers, sons and daughters who use health care today."

~ Rosemary Gibson, of the Robert Wood Johnson Foundation and author of *The Wall of Silence.*

"Mary Ellen Mannix respectfully reveals some of the painful truths of medicine and law through the poignant example of her child, his brief but head-on collision with our healthcare system, and her very personal journey finding strength deep in tragedy, and emerging with a voice that will no doubt help countless patients in the future. *Split the Baby* will open your eyes, break your heart and raise your spirit. This powerful little book should be mandatory reading in medical and law school, and is also a must-read for every health care provider, officer of the court, and anyone who sincerely cares about patient safety and doctor-patient communication."

Nicholas A. DiNubile, MD
Renowned orthopaedic surgeon, chosen in "Best Doctors in America ", best selling author of *FrameWork- Your 7 Step Program for Healthy Muscles, Bones and Joints*, and Executive Producer and host of the award winning PBS special *Your Body's FrameWork*.

Acknowledgements

Of all the writing, editing and re-editing that has happened around this little book, this part is the most difficult to finalize. Since this book really started eight years ago when I first wrote a note to the hospital, every person who has patiently stood witness to the grief and my hope for something good to come of tragedy has helped to create this book. There is no way I could list or remember everyone by name. The story is full of hard truths and difficult questions. In its midst are a multitude of blessings found in the people who were able to help find answers and offer peace. This book is, in effect, an exercise in hope and gratitude.

Jim Beasley, Sr. died a year before we went to trial. Connecting with him was not by my design but was the influence of some greater force or being – whether he would have ascribed to that argument or not, I know it is true. Jim Beasley Jr. offered legal expertise, representation and a level of compassion rarely seen, or at least acknowledged, in the legal profession. I have said thank you to Jim many times and I still haven't said it enough. His wife, Liz, has also been a source of inspiration and comfort. I am grateful for all she has been willing to share with me while enduring her own tragic loss.

Dr. Nick fielded my calls and inquiries about health care issues for years and still does. Running from surgery, in between patients, or while at the skate park with his son, he will answer my calls as earnestly as any family member and yet he is a friend. To me, he is like a favorite big brother. I owe a certain level of gratitude for the other physicians and caregivers in this book that would eventually answer my request for a personal conversation. Dr. Lazaros Kochilas is a uniquely compassionate person and talented physician. Despite the events that led us to meet and though we surely wish the events discussed here had never happened, I am grateful for the personal conversations we shared post-verdict. Hopefully after reading our story, other patients and physicians will not wait so long for transparent, honest, compassionate dialogues. Thank you also to the healthcare providers and lawyers working towards improving our healthcare system by acknowledging its humanity.

There is an invisible army of families and patients affected by preventable medical errors working to encourage transparency in healthcare to save future patients from harm. The first I met on this front Jeni Dingman and Ilene Corina, introduced me to many more who would help shape my mission. Thank you. I am also grateful for the work, encouragement, conversation and friendship of Becky Martins, Helen Haskell, Patty Skolnik, Bill Wright, Bill Thiel, Rosemary Gibson, and Jim Conway.

I have been blessed with an extensive extended family. To each of them, I am thankful for you regardless of where we have been, where we are or where we will be.

I am grateful for the moms of Christopher Gabaree Jr., Dylan Bernard, Anthony Crawford, Thomas Turner, Lauren, Angelique, Carlos, Kadin, Michael, Lewis, Katie, Cayman and many more children who passed as their life had just begun. These moms walked beside me and held me up.

Thanks to the entire West Hill School community that showed me laughter is a wonderful medicine. Thanks to classmates in my master's program who listened to my angst and anxiety to restore healing in health care. Specifically those classmates who encouraged me to share this story in book form. In particular, I am grateful for my Education track peers - Deanna Webb, Gloria Alvarez Poulson, Kevin Eisenhart, and Paul Malecki who really are Masters in restoring healing. Though not a classmate, Ralph Cipriano was like a teacher. I learned a great deal about the writing process thanks to his generous sharing of time and talent. Thanks also to our church family at Our Mother of Good Counsel, Bryn Mawr, PA for their gentle caring through the rough waters.

I am most grateful for the viewpoints that my children, Emily, Sam, Grace, and Patrick, have shared and for their strength to endure life with fractured parents. My surviving children are an inspiration for their resilience and unconditional love. They are my heroes. I am eternally grateful for their patience and understanding. And Michael, among all the other things, thank you for driving the van on the way home from the hospital October 13th, 2001. I never would have made it home (or here) without you.

~ Mary Ellen

In memory

James Matthew Mannix   10/2 - 13/01

&

Thomas Evan James Beasley   9/25/03

"I do not want the peace that passeth understanding.

I want the understanding which bringeth peace."

– Helen Keller

Preface

Losing a child always changes your perspective. Always. Mary Ellen's book takes you through her happiest days turned to her worst nightmare. And it does it in a very personal way that makes the experience all the more palpable and revealing.

When you've lost a child, you feel alone, without answers. Questions and guilt flood every pore in your body. The unbearable pain and confusion makes you withdraw. Mary Ellen powered through these crippling emotions to get answers. She describes these feelings in a way that only a Mother who has lost a child can express. My Dad and I were privileged enough to receive the phone call from Mary Ellen when she began her journey that put this book in your hands. For more than four years we worked together to find out what happened to her little boy, and we did. The process took us around the east coast of the United States and through many pages of medical records, articles, reports, and stories (some more true than others). Then, it took us, and the health care system that failed James, to trial in one of the more hostile venues in the country. Even with a substantial offer, Mary Ellen didn't use this process, or her loss, as a means of self-pity or to line her pockets. Mary Ellen's silence wouldn't be bought by the hospital or the physicians in exchange for a confidential settlement, even when times were tough. That's because Mary Ellen's character drove her to use this pain, sadness and loss as a means to help others. Her story is heartbreaking, inspiring, and one that everyone in health care needs to read. This book is also a necessary read for any family that has had to persevere through the unthinkable.

Since you're reading this preface, you've obviously found something about this book that piqued your interest. I encourage you to make the time to explore this book and experience all of the insights it provides. As counselor and friend to Mary Ellen, I'm proud to have been part of her courageous trek for answers, which has blossomed into an unending quest to improve health care for all.

~ Jim Beasley, Jr.

Split the Baby:

One Child's Journey through Medicine and Law

Part I

I know what I have given you. I do not know
what you have received."

~ Antonio Porchia

I walked away from $750,000. It was not a difficult decision, nor one that has left regret. The only things it could have produced were grave blankets and a gag. However, what could it restore?

Money was never a very good motivator. It never really impressed me. I have always been a teacher, not a judge or jury. Those that had money were measured by what they did, not how much it had. It is certainly not that I didn't understand the need for it and the high cost of living in an affluent city suburb with four growing children – one within two years of college. However, I never really got the hang of hanging onto money. There was always someone or something that needed it more. There is no need to swing anything to hit someone who knows I am bad with it. Do even less and you'll trip over someone I owe. The intent is always to repay. The realization of said intent is painfully slow as life adds on more expenses while taking away zeroes.

When given this duty to consider the cost of my convictions, I was three weeks post total abdominal hysterectomy. Coverage for which had come in question since my husband, the insured subscriber, had without warning lost his job just weeks before the scheduled, medically necessary surgery. Our rent was well past due. We sold the only house we ever owned. Its proceeds paid off bills that quickly accumulated in the shadows of October 2001. Just a couple months previous, it took a sheriff's deputy at my door to remind me of the intent to catch up on a year old oil-heating bill. The food that only occasionally filled the cabinets (most often, there were more empty cabinets than cereal boxes) was at times from our church pantry. All of these red marks on my credit did come to mind during my deliberation of this large medical malpractice settlement for the death of my son. It was another one of those beautiful spotlessly blue-sky, early autumns Saturday mornings. There were many like it in 2001. I never needed direction to relive the first two weeks of that month. The most serious consideration for selling out became the strongest for pushing onward. If I did not accept the offer, I would have to spend my son's birthday, a Sunday, at the lawyer's office preparing for trial on Monday. We were back in the days and moments of the events, that led to this proposed jackpot by calendar date, if not by mother's memory.

Four years out from the shattering event, I thought we should be more independent and not have to ask for help. It was obscure that a bank account could be so empty in a four bedroom, two and half bath single. When we moved in the luxuries seemed affordable. What was missing from the budget plan was the challenge of two heads of household with fractured attention spans and already stretched finances. When this large sum came across my path, our sole subsistence was part time jobs and no benefits. With four living children to support, some may judge my decision to leave three quarters of a million dollars on the table as irresponsible. It is an obvious argument. It was what I had already lost and would have to relinquish that made the six digits diminutive and inconsequential in comparison.

"Babies are the greatest of all God's gifts."

~ Unknown

I was just finishing a shower when there was a knock at the door. It was nondescript, neither forceful nor melodic. If only I had sensed the urgency to it, I would have seen the doctor's face before he spoke even a word. Perhaps, I would have understood the gravity of the information he was about to share. Perhaps that could have been the thing to prepare me for the next few hours. The knock, however, seemed as meaningless as any other did from a neighbor, co-worker, or a lavatory companion that had gone unrecalled before it. That it was on a hospital room door was not even alarming. I had never had a reason to feel unsafe in a healthcare setting.

Muffled voices made their way through the closed bathroom door. I knew one was from my husband. I could not imagine to whom he was speaking. It seemed plausible a family member could have decided to pop in after visiting hours. I hurried. I did not want to miss anything. As I came out of the bathroom and turned, a tall, slender man in a white lab coat stood with hands clenched by his sides. A young blonde-haired woman stood beside him with her gaze focused on him. No, this was not family. Having set forth some base information to my husband, the white coated foreigner regretfully then repeated everything to me, the mom.

I remember the deep breath he took, which made time pass more slowly. There must have been some introduction. I had never seen this person before and his words were the key to a permanent place in my memory. This had one key in and nothing to free it. He was polite, soft-spoken, yet his words were full of accent and woe. He glanced at me as he spoke. I would have had to sit on the floor and to his left to force eye contact.

"Mrs. Mannix, there has been a sudden event."

I could not understand. I looked to my husband who was, just as the nurse, speechless and leaving responsibility to the white lab coat.

"What do you mean? What happened?"

"Your son, James, has had a serious event. It was very sudden."

"Can I see him?"

"It is very serious."

"What happened?"

The blonde-haired woman spoke up. "It was during rounds. We were all right there." It was a feeble attempt to relieve a mother's guilt. I never considered she was trying to relieve her own. The doctor rubbed his fingers against each other as his hands balled into two fists at the end of his arms on each side of the white coat.

"It was a very sudden and very serious event. They are working on him now."

Serious. Sudden. Event. Event. Event. Event. Event. Event.

Sudden. I did not like this word.

So much frustration enveloped me as I froze with an uncomfortable stillness. How could I understand of what this stranger was talking? What words should I string together and in what order? I struggled for some comprehension of what the physician's mantra meant. How could I get him to speak in a way I could understand? Thunderstruck, I meekly and with a sense of embarrassment at having to repeat myself again asked, "What happened?" There was no additional detail given. If another word were offered in answer perhaps, I would have formed a different question.

I failed. I taxed my vocabulary to ask the same question in many different ways, the answer remained constant.

"Your son has had a serious event."

His body language did not change course. The hands. The hands kept their own rhythm. Unaccustomed to trusting my maternal instincts in an environment where they were never before tested, I could not even imagine what these hands had done. The fingers massaged each other with the thumb as leader. Like a well-rehearsed marching band, they closed together in a four count around their leader and chorused again. It was rhythmic, tense and peculiar. Not until all the pieces were revealed, did I understand the lyrical movements. Just a new doctor to me, years would pass before learning how intimately this man already knew my baby. The hands were representatives for the walnut-sized heart and soul it encapsulated just moments before our meeting. He and the blonde left saying they would call when I could go to my baby.

Their visit left me with a strong, palpable, disconcerting anxiety. The kind that wants you to do something. The kind that either ascribes everything to memory or removes everything. The kind that does not allow the body to remain but produces no meaningful result. Collapse is within reason. Adrenaline is surging. The mind is coursing through an uncontrollable series of bad thoughts yet each one unproven and unmatched to the true horror. The lessons of a life lived in dutiful submission and unearned respect for white-coats stubbornly resistant to change. Over the next several hours, the anxiety robbed me of all knowledge, ideals, confidence, and belief I ever held.

In shock and stupidity, I stood there. Like an obedient child, I did not move. I had no control, no way to communicate, no knowledge, no rights. I felt naked, exposed, and almost as vulnerable as a newborn baby in a cardiac intensive care unit. I reverted to the lessons learned in Catholic grade school.

Pray.

Trust.

Hope.

Be good and nothing bad will happen.

Do an act of contrition. Say a hundred in case it was something I did that was causing punishment to my baby.

I wanted to run to James. I could probably have made it before security got to me. Two nurses' stations, four corridors, and two sets of double doors would to have been breached. Fear and helplessness kept me from moving. The curse of hindsight gave me more guilt than that which successfully kept me still in the first place. What would have happened if I demanded to see my son? Why was I so easily led?

A lifetime hung in the balance.

In nature, there's no blemish

But the mind;

None can be called deform'd

But the unkind."

from "Twelfth Night" by William Shakespeare

This pregnancy, as much as those that came before it, was a surprise. No longer young and inexperienced, I knew the hurdles of an unexpected pregnancy would be followed by immeasurable joy. Immediately, I followed medical advice. The long-standing relationship I had formed with the father and son obstetric team had spanned eleven years and three children already. The sense of family dedication spanning generations was reassuring to me as a young mother. Though the office changed over time – the father had retired and the son had to expand to include many other physicians – the assurances received early were held tightly. The nurse and receptionist became extensions of my family. It was without much thought that I obliged his office earlier that year by forwarding letters to my state representative about the plight of doctors against a fierce medical malpractice system. I was as much invested in their survival as if I was a physician myself. It was a relief that my OB would be allowed to deliver babies again starting just a few short months before my expected delivery date. The cost of liability insurance had become prohibitive for him in the previous few years. There was not much that I would not have done for him. When he asked me for my understanding while he closed his office to march in Harrisburg, I obliged. When the OB said to get an ultrasound I only asked where and when.

The ultrasound doctor said to get a fetal echocardiogram. The cardiologist said come back for another echocardiogram. Accepting orders and excelling as a dutiful soldier, I marched to the tune prescribed. There was more prenatal activity with this one but there was also very little concern. All the medical providers were harmonious in the instruction not to worry. After the second echocardiogram, the cardiologist, Dr. Bhat, determined this non-issue issue was the development of the baby's aorta, the great vessel leaving the heart, which carries oxygen-rich blood to the body. I called him later the same day and asked, "Can you spell that?"

"C-o-a-r-c-t-a-t-i-o-n of the aorta."

Dr. Bhat said to let him know when the baby would be delivered since a diagnosis couldn't be confirmed until shortly after birth.

"What's shortly?" I inquired.

"A few hours after delivery."

The OB, Dr. Chastenay, said that I was receiving guidance from a heart facility with the "best baby heart doctor around." Many others would echo that impression over the following two months. I trusted them. If there were information that would be detrimental to my baby, certainly someone would share it.

I visited the facility despite carrying the companion of detachment. I was going through motions that some other high-risk pregnant mom should be doing but was not. I assumed some guilt for taking precious time and attention away from important, expert, caring and selfless medical providers that should be spent on another parent and child with bigger problems than mine should. I was most likely wasting the facility's time as well as my own. After a tour of the facility by the social worker, I was surprised to be sitting in the office and meeting with the head of Nemours Cardiac Center, the world-renowned surgeon, Dr. William I. Norwood. Of course, I had never heard of him. My husband and I waited. Upon arrival in his office, Dr. Norwood sat in a large chair and threw an unopened chart on his desk. He told us that he hadn't viewed our son's echocardiograms or the written reports but would concur with whatever Dr. Bhat said. Perhaps, that was our baby's file that he had just flung on the oversized dark wood desk but I couldn't be sure.

Dr. Bhat had performed a second fetal echocardiogram on August 13 2001. At the conclusion of the procedure, Dr. Bhat sat with me in a small, empty room. He drew a rough diagram of what he believed was the concern for my unborn child's health. He told me "we're not talking open heart surgery here." There were three possible options for treatment - medication therapy, angioplasty (a "balloon through a catheter") of which he drew a diagram for my nonprofessional's ignorance, or a corrective surgery a bit later. That was what Dr. Bhat said so the message from Norwood was that he would not be performing open-heart surgery. That this was not as big a deal as what some other parents and children face. When you go to the dentist and see the pictures on the walls of children with their front teeth rotted out and you're told your child has one cavity that can be treated in the next visit, there's a sense of guilt but relief. Even when there is need of further dental procedures, comparatively speaking, there is gratitude.

I immediately discounted any discussion Dr. Norwood shared -especially when he drew a line with his finger down the middle of his chest. I had no idea what that charade-like action meant. Nor, did I understand that it was an important element of our discussion. The meeting was wrapped up quickly. There was certainly no need to waste the surgeon's time. Clearly, we wouldn't need him.

Perhaps, my naiveté was the 9/11-effect. I met Norwood for the first time the week before this international time marker. As I was working to settle any maternal instincts, this national tragedy hit. As a mom and teacher, I focused on restoring faith and balance for the children in my life. This new life I carried was one of my tools.

Tragedy and sorrow had filled every pore of the northeasterners existence at that time. Anguish and suffering had engulfed thousands of families. Cars in train station parking lots were not moved for months. Stories of parentless children flooded the media. Even worse were the stories of parents who had lost children. Disconcerting still were the parents worried their children would be shipped off to fight an enemy that had no headquarters. My children asked repeatedly that September, "Are we at war?" "Will we be okay?" "What will happen to us?"

My full belly reassured our little middle class American family that life would go on and survival was God-guaranteed. Alternatively, my ignorance was just that - my own ignorance. Years later, defense counsel would work hard to exploit that naivete and make me appear both unreasonably ignorant and frighteningly conniving.

But one thing follows another.

Things were different inside my mother.

Padded and jolly I would ride

The perfect comfort of her inside.

They tuck me in a rustling bed

-     *I lie there, raging, small, and red.*
I may sleep soon, I may forget,

But I won't forget that I regret.

Thom Gunn (1929-), excerpts from "Baby Song"

OCTOBER 2, 2001

James was bigger than expected, screamed a loud, raspy hello, had all ten fingers and ten toes, and was perfect in every way. He was the only one of my children that I truly felt move through me and into the world. The first hands to hold him were not mine. He received a full work up from blue scrubs that were asked to be nearby for the delivery of a child with a possible prenatal coarctation of the aorta diagnosis.

"8 pounds 4 ounces."

"20 and half inches."

"Congratulations. Here is your son. He's perfect," the nurse confidently remarked as she placed him in my arms. Typical mother, I fell in love instantly. The way his mouth moved and his deep, sea blue eyes worked to focus. I was his world. My firm yet gentle embrace was meant to offer reassurance. He was pink, rosy, awake, squirming and rooting. Before I could do my own digit count, a nurse without pardon began to take him from me. With a quick jerk, I pulled back.

"We just need to take him to the neonatal intensive care unit and do the echo. He'll be right back." She spoke as if I should have known this already and I wondered if I should have. I leaned away from her and toward my husband.

"Michael, you take him down. I will be okay if you are with him. One of us needs to be with him."

The once overcrowded delivery room became cavernous. Five minutes after delivering my son, I was alone. In all the planning by expectant parents for the delivery, never are there plans for finding company or activity for the new mom just after delivery. That is a universal expectation – she will be holding the baby or tended to by doctors, nurses, midwives, new grandmothers, or husbands. I stared out the large plate glass window. It was late afternoon. A crisp blue inviting sky pulled me in. The past few months' advice of the medical personnel replayed reminders: "Don't worry. This is not a problem. Coarct babies come home quickly. We are not talking open heart." It would be sinful to think I had a bigger problem than anyone else, let alone the woman down the hall using volume to entice her baby out.

Michael returned empty-handed. Though he asked, the medical team did not allow him to stay while they performed an echo on his newborn son. We would be called as soon as we could get James. To hasten a reunion, we busied with getting squared away on the maternity floor. We phoned the older children. An interminably long three hours passed without any word from the people that took our baby. Via wheel chair, I headed unannounced to the NICU. As I entered, a red-haired physician stopped me in the doorway. She introduced herself as the pediatric cardiologist who performed the echocardiogram. Dr. Gibbons congratulated us and said she had arranged transport for our son to go to the children's hospital.

I jumped out of the wheelchair. Someone made a feeble attempt to remind me to be self-conscious from the rear since I was still in a hospital gown. The pressing issue was a new baby traveling without a mother. Transport without discussion was completely unexpected.

The parent/physician discussion that followed was interrupted by the arrival of our older children at the NICU room door. Juggling the excitement and concern of 4, 9, and 11 year olds with the foreign instructions of a specialist while trying to get acquainted with the new baby proved a winning combination for the medical team. After hearing, "not a problem," "don't worry," and, "If this was my child, it is where I would want him to be," we acquiesced. All the while James lay there, awake, flexing his arms to display the strength he would utilize sooner than expected. He cooed. He was hungry. His color was rosy from his head to the farthest toes. He wanted to eat. He wanted to be held. He got neither.

It certainly was not ideal to watch the NICU nurses and medical transport personnel try to put an IV in a new baby for an infusion of prostaglandins. Prostaglandins was the medication that would keep the prenatal circulatory system open, which would buy time as we decided how to best proceed. "Oh, he's a hard stick," was the medical team's consensus. He lay there looking at me as I talked him through it. He tried to pull away and was successful a couple of times. I was okay though. I had my job to do. It seemed to be working. I was keeping him calm for an extended period as the medical providers just kept failing at theirs. Not one was able to get in the IV. The staff sent me away again. I returned to the previously tended hospital room with family minus one. There, we reassured others' concerns. We not only allowed for optimism, we encouraged it. The children argued over the potential costume for the newest to parade on Halloween at month's end. The kids shared school news and disagreed on who could bring James to school first.

During my son's fifth hour, he was taken to another hospital. His father followed. His brother and sisters went home disappointed for not being allowed by the medical team to hold their new brother. It was the first and last time they ever saw him.

Alone for the first time in nine months, I struggled. Company was found in the literature from the children's hospital. I replenished my fluids was a meager attempt to silence the metal cradles full of round young lives being wheeled into their new moms' arms. At 4AM, there was little to help me sleep. I called the children's hospital CICU. Though surprised to be receiving such a late call from a parent, the nurse was still pleasant. She thought he was "so cute" and "just beautiful." The nurse shared not a nary of worry, only reassurance as to his excellent condition. "James is the healthiest kid down here right now. " She was also confident about the importance of my recovery because, as I would hear many, many times, "Coarct babies come home quickly."

At the time, I was uncomfortably ignorant of my son's condition. As a preschool teacher, I had not utilized the internet often. We had only recently gotten access at home anyway. I had to wait to use my husband's work laptop to search the phrase. Unlike the issues I had faced previously as a mom – proper academic challenges, bullying, friendships and neighborhood politics – I had no preparation or familiarity with congenital heart defects. I had learned that a coarctation of the aorta (COA) is included in the long list of known congenital heart defects. I had learned that diagnosed and managed properly, the coarctation would not limit or shorten my son's life. I had learned, via this internet search, that some undiagnosed Coarct patients had lived into their forties. Though that was certainly alarming, it was also reassuring; I would have time to make sure my son got the appropriate care to live well past his forties.

My grandmother, for whom I am named, offered forty-two grandchildren to the world. By the time I began a family, many of those forty-two were already well on their way to continue Irish Catholic family traditions themselves. Yet, not one had ever been targeted with a birth defect. My stomach searched for the calm that the medical team and family maintained. It arrived at a compromise. The outside looked fine; my insides were fighting back emotional anarchy. Of all the amazing combinations of words in the English language, those two words - birth & defect - offered more anxiety than any I had ever before experienced as a mother. Just two days later, "sudden event" would steal the distinction.

Though I was a relatively frequent visitor to an obstetrician's office (three older children and one previous miscarriage), a congenital heart defect had never ever been part of the doctor- patient discussions. Which I assumed, must mean it is a rarity. An appropriate degree of worry accompanied it. Yet, to each person that knew more than I did,

I had nothing to worry about but my own recovery. My worries were no more important than the worries of someone else. Had the time allowed, I would have searched as far as possible to educate myself on the condition without consuming the physician and nurse's time. I would have learned what many of the medical team told me, "Coarctation of the aorta is one of the most easily treated CHDs." I also would have discovered that CHDs are the most common and deadliest form of birth defect. Children with a severe coarctation don't eat much and sleep a lot. Babies born with a CHD are usually smaller. Most born with a CHD have more than one anomaly – whether cardiac or otherwise. In those born with multiple CHDs, the first (and least complicated) issue corrected is the coarctation.

After fifty years of pediatric cardiology and cardiovascular surgery, the procedures to repair a coarctation are well practiced and not experimental. Most children born with a coarctation of the aorta and die of it have not been diagnosed. The condition catches the happy new parents and many pediatricians by surprise. After days of not eating well and sleeping all the time, a parent of an undiagnosed COA will call the pediatrician's office where very often they are told by well-meaning albeit ignorant nursing staff, "Oh, when the baby is hungry, the baby will eat." "You are not trying hard enough to wake him every two hours." When the parent tries explaining on the phone that the child's breathing seems very shallow, the triage on the other side of the line will remind the parent that "All new babies breathe like that. A new baby's breathing rate is faster too." Moreover, the line (or some rendition) that kicks the field goal, "You're new at this. Calm down, your baby is fine." All too often, a follow up call is made directly to 911 when the baby is found blue in the crib. The scene of a new father trying to maintain an emotional distance while pushing down hard on his newborn's sternum through a teddy bear covered cotton onesie is unbearable for most to imagine. The commonwealth of Pennsylvania has mandated that every newborn receive a screening for hearing before the baby leave the hospital. There is no requirement for CHD testing.

Only one of the many known CHDs, coarctation diagnosis was found to be uncomplicated. A well-known cardiologist from the mid-20th century found an easy, inexpensive way to test for it. Coarctation of the aorta is a narrowing of the large vessel leaving the heart that provides oxygenated blood to the lower body. Blood pressure in a coarct baby is high in the upper extremities and low in the lower extremities. Dr. Bernard Levine correctly hypothesized that if one compresses both the big toe and thumb at the same time, and then relieve the pressure, the resultant blanching would last longer in the toe. The examining physician only needs ten seconds and a stethoscope (Lown). A more modern way to check oxygenation is the pulse oximetry externally attached to a finger or toe.

These were not my concerns. In the first year of the new century, James's physicians didn't have to rely on a stopwatch and exterior examination. The benefit of modern technology confirmed the prenatal diagnosis. An echocardiogram utilizes ultrasound technology. A view of the inside of the chest is created without incision – not too unlike a sonogram for pregnancy. Even if I had all the signs and symptoms to look for, James did not show them. James was the biggest baby I had, he ate without falling asleep, and he was not bluish like other "heart babies."

The interior view of James showed a narrowing of the great vessel at a point that limited the blood flow to the lower portion of his body. Because of the extra work, his right ventricle was slightly enlarged. This condition would need treatment. The birthday video and one made the next day would serve as his physicians' guide to treatment. They decided on surgery. James, his dad and I were not given options for care. We were not told the risks of surgery. I was never told they were about to perform open-heart surgery on my two-day-old.

James's situation was one that most moms of coarct babies would envy. He was being diagnosed and cared for before going home. However, the only knowledge that I had gained up until that night was reassurance from the obstetrician, pediatrician and a couple MD acquaintances that I was seeking medical treatment in the best pediatric cardiac center in the world. One reason gave this elite distinction – the cardiac center director and surgeon. However, my newly postpartum intellect did not allow for consideration that my baby might be staring down a scalpel. Monitoring. He would simply be monitored until I could follow. Therefore, I worked to maintain calm. I worked to push away the thoughts of loneliness and separation. For me, it would be brief and temporary. Every mother is inherently aware of the possibility of not bringing home a newborn. That is the worst fear, recognized by all; realized by fewer.

The stillness made for a long night.

"You may house their bodies

but not their souls,
For their souls dwell

in the house of tomorrow,
which you cannot visit,

not even in your dreams."

From "On Children," Khalil Gibran

October 3, 2001

James and I were reunited twenty-four hours later.
Lying in bed #5 of the CICU, he was free to be held with just
the one IV invading him. Evidently, without us present the
medical team had placed the prostaglandins IV into his scalp.
The drug Prostaglandins was utilized to keep his circulation
working the way it worked before birth. It helped to ensure
that his Coarct wouldn't give him any problems before repair.
At least he was receiving the medication that would keep his in
utero circulatory system flowing. I sat in the rocking chair and
quickly swaddled him with the soft cotton hospital blanket. We
began where we left off - a gentle but firm grasp to offer
reassurance and safety in the strange bright world. He gazed
my way and his mouth moved in earnest to eat and speak.
Clearly, he had a lot to tell me. First, he should eat.

"I would like to breast feed him. The lactation
consultant at the other hospital said there would be concern to
document his intake and output," I began to inform the nurse.

Quickly the nurse interrupted, "Exactly - so you can't
do that."

I pressed on, "but if we get a clean diaper on him now,
weigh him, feed him and then weigh him and his diaper
after..."

"No, I am sorry. Here is the bottle."

I took the bottle with resignation but resolve that as
soon as possible he would be breastfed. He ate, was awake,
and fell asleep. He was just so little. All 8 pounds and 4 ounces

of him. It had been over a day since we were together. It felt like a lifetime. That entire first day of his life, I had missed. It would be his sentence to live his young life without family by his side. For those few precious moments, he had shared smiles, coos, and soft touches. He drank a few ounces of formula from the plain baby bottle.

Uninvited, a new physician pulled up a chair. She had short dark hair, wore blue scrubs, and took up space next to the isolette. She introduced herself as part of the surgeon's team. It was her assignment to go over the consent form with us. Simple. Not to worry. Do this all the time. Dr. Spurrier, an anesthesiologist, was to get consent. She had in her hand two 8 x 11" pieces of white photocopied paper. I listened while studying the baby.

He looked beautiful despite the one lead from his head. "I asked to breastfeed him," I began to tell her. She concurred with whatever the staff said.

I held him. I held him.

Cradled in my arms with his head nestled in the crook of my left arm. I stroked his soft downy scalp with my right hand. Slowly starting from his forehead my hand gently smoothed his downy wisps of dark hair. His body responded as he nestled down deeper into the space between my heart and arms. The pacifier moved up and down in his mouth furiously as he gently peered at me leaning his head to the right. I sang softly with my head cocked down to the left. We were one again. Mother and baby. For just one moment, I was confident we were in the right place - with each other. Heaven on earth.

I held my baby tighter. He readjusted and looked for food. I obliged with the bottle in hand. Just a few minutes had elapsed. "Do you have any other questions?"

Michael and I looked at each other in the hopes that we were not missing anything. We held blank stares, as this was a new topic. Neither one of us had any familiarity. Given the clear instruction that if we did not consent to their recommended treatments our son wouldn't "make it," trust was the only option.

Still getting to know him, my eyes and my thoughts were affixed. The insecure thoughts that never had invaded my relationship with my older children until they went to their first babysitter or first day of preschool or first parent-free play date were not only confusing but also a cause for mental disorganization. I was only confident holding James.

Again, she stated more than asked, "Any questions at all."

I tried to remember the few conversations from the previous months. The memories were of reassurance and confidence. Nothing to worry about, easy, 100% recovery rate (Dr. Norwood had actually laughed when asked what is the survival rate), not open-heart surgery, general anesthesia. Each of which was a concern, but did not warrant a thriving mini-drama.

The previous 24 hours of doctors had gone over some scenarios with my husband. The focus of questions the evening before were, "What exactly do you want us to do?"

"How long will it take?"

"When can we be with him?"

The only question I asked was the same I asked the surgeon a month prior, "Is there anything you do beyond general anesthesia that I should know?"

"No," was again the definitive response.

The papers were handed to my husband since my arms were full. He signed, with my support, the paper headed: "repair of coarctation of the aorta."

Dental forms had more detail. In October 2001 inside A. I. Du Pont Hospital for Children, you could find handouts and wall size postings that read: "Your child's rights and your responsibilities."

The third right was to have all the options for our child's care told to us along with risks of the procedure as well as the risks of not doing it. After reading the hospital literature, learning that the surgeon was world renowned and he had a procedure named after him, I felt James's care would be of high quality. Much of the institution's literature was dotted with The Joint Commission's stamp of approval. Any quality hospital had that accrediting body's name on their literature. All of the safety precautions and oversight possibilities were surely in place and in practice.

After Dr. Spurrier left, I put the bottle down and picked up my son's pacifier, gently rubbing it against his lips. He received it easily and with eyes closed, head leaning to the left, he fell asleep. The weight of his body was full but light. My arm needed the extra support from the rocking chair. I gingerly pulled the terry hospital blanket from under my am and slipped it around his head. It was alarming to see a needle protrude through his scalp and it would be more so if I accidentally pulled it out. However, my concerns were still to keep him warm and swaddled. Every brand new baby is quieted by attempts to replicate the tightness and warmth found within mom. Once I had maneuvered the blanket around the back of his head and shoulders, a corner was tucked in under his arm. A second corner was pulled up from his feet and pulled together with the corner farthest from me. Everything was tucked in between my son's peach fuzzed shoulder and my white t-shirt. He nestled deeper. I allowed the gentle rocking of the chair to soothe us back into the security of each other. Eyes closed, we were alone and in peace amidst white lights and a sterile environment.

In slumber, the pacifier slipped out of James's mouth and rolled against my forearm, gently sending me an important reminder. The precariousness of fatigue while sitting in a wooden chair over a linoleum floor with a newborn was a hazard. After a few more moments, I sacrificed. Carefully as to not stir him, I stood up and placed him in the isolette. I kept him swaddled. Then, I watched him sleep, caressing his head, cheeks, tummy, arms and fingers. Though I had to, I didn't want to leave. With a kiss to his forehead wishing him sweet dreams, I left him in a bright room with strangers as his trusted bedfellows. I let him rest.

"The older I get the less I rush to judgment.

The less I rush, the older my patients get."

"The Lost Art of Healing"

By Dr. Bernard Lown

October 4, 2001

Overnight I visited but missed his "fussy-time." The pacifier helped in staving off his hunger. James was resting peacefully. As much as I wanted to hold him, I dare not disturb a sleeping baby who would be undergoing a medical procedure in a short few hours. After another hour of admiring him quietly, I left again as the staff asked for privacy during rounds. I would return with my husband shortly before the operation.

Returning to the CICU in daylight did not relieve any tension. Exercise was always a welcome relief for increased tension and worry. This was not so early on the morning of October 4. The walk was full of fear. There is never any worry for the unknown except when it suddenly becomes your new normal. It was like walking blind and not knowing the terrain. My breathing was rapid. I held his hand, hoping for an extension to courage and calm. Enough was granted that as I walked the long corridor, I could see the soft lights radiating from the corner of my eyes. Peaceful tones and gentle music emanated. Calm was present. These rooms we walked past were full of parents and much sicker but recovering well children. I yearned for these tomorrows. At an attempt to accept that my worries were surely less than others, I tried small talk. I acted as if this was a normal morning two days after a child's birth. There was much to look forward to after the procedure. We would be taking him home. The hospital was such a foreign place. Maybe I should make heart-shaped birth announcements. Maybe tiny scrubs for Halloween. Conversation quickly quieted. I had no knowledge of the common language and acceptable customs of a children's hospital.

It was easy to read what was posted. "Please wash hands before visiting in the CICU." There was a small sink and soap available to the right as you entered the CICU double - doors. As soon as we walked in, we could see our son as his was the bed directly across from the entrance. He was some fifty feet away. I wanted to run and pick him up but I also acknowledged that he was in a threatened position - in a hospital under the care of trained medical providers. This was their arena and I would oblige every request. Therefore, I took the moments long enough to sing "Happy Birthday" to properly sterilize my hands. A technique taught in my preschool classroom. I was anxious to see and touch James. I was interrupted on my way to him as the surgeon came to us at the sink. He wanted to know if we had any more questions. I asked again, "What will you be doing?"

"We will cut away the section that is narrowed and widen it with a graft (or a patch, or something to that extent)."

I asked again, "Is there anything else I need to know?"

"No."

I asked him to pray and said I would be praying for him. "Thank you," I said more beseechingly than appreciatively. He needed to understand how important this child was for many people. This doctor had to be careful and successful in whatever he was about to do. Dr. Norwood quickly pulled his hand away, without a word turned, and walked way. He was not impressed with my gentle plea.

Another anesthesiologist escorted my husband, James, and I to the operating room. James was still beautiful. He wore a full face, distinctively shaped eyebrows, perfect button nose, and pink rosy color. I brushed his arm and placed my finger in his hands. There was little reaction as he had already received medication to relax him during the procedure. Letting him go alone with strangers into a giant room full of equipment felt like I had in that moment failed as a parent. Was there some other check, question, request, authorization I was supposed to do, find, give? It felt so wrong. He didn't seem as sick as we were being told. Yet, I was not medically trained. I dismissed my instincts and pushed away bad thoughts. This was a time to be positive.

As time passed, I stayed in our assigned room and waited for the promised updates. A call at 7:30 said they had started. By 9:30, "he is on bypass now."

I stopped breathing.

The caller realized my shock and volunteered, "That's okay. It is part of the procedure."

Around 10:00, the final call, again from the same social worker that gave us a tour a month earlier was, "he is off bypass now and they are closing him. We will let you know when you can come see him."

For about three hours, I was locked in this room. It seemed like days. The room was stationed just above the hospital day care center. It was a good distraction for me. As a preschool teacher and former, day care center director I was able to observe the activities. A blond child wandered away from the group. Her destination was the fence that enclosed her day's playground. With no easy gate in sight, she began to climb. I watched anxiously waiting to see a staff member notice. It seemed an interminable delay before she was noticed and redirected. Another child was pulled by her right arm off a slide. She looked like a rag doll in a terrier's grasp. I wondered to whom I would report all the deficient care. Surely, I was watching the children of those working to save my child.

Just beyond the day care center was a wide-open field and sky. It was a beautiful sky blue. Just occasionally interrupted by a small white puff. During the Fall of 2001, the lost souls of 9/11 seemed to be doing all they could to keep the skies they perished in beautiful and reassuring for those below.

Finally at 11:30 am the call came. Barely setting down the receiver Michael and I were out the door and washing up in the CICU. We were met there by Dr. Norwood, who was quite pleased. "You'll be home by Monday, Tuesday at the latest and he can be playing football when he gets older like any other child."

"So everything went as you planned."

"Yes, there were no surprises. He is doing well," the surgeon proclaimed.

With a lighter step, I walked back to my new baby. He was not so new anymore. A scar ran down the center of his chest from under his neck to his belly. A tube protruding from the bottom of the scar ran down the length and height of his bed into a rectangular shaped clear plastic container. It bubbled and percolated as an overgrown coffeemaker my mother once used. Though mostly clear, there was an occasional tinge of red. His nose was invaded by a clear tube attached to a larger accordion clear plastic tube connected to a large contraption that was plugged into the wall. A catheter ran from the diaper barely on him. A white clothespin pinched his finger. A variety of other wires and lines decorated him like an unwilling Christmas tree, topped with gold sticker in the shape of a heart.

Our time was brief. Just long enough for a touch of my hand to his tiny fingers and my lips to his chubby foot. The staff reiterated the importance of his rest and their presence to watch him closely. The cardiac center staff told Michael and I that our newborn son needed to remain calm and not become excited by the voice of a parent. Perhaps, I considered, they would let me stay if I promised not to speak. There are times when a person who is ill of body or quite low in spirit needs a quiet companion. Nothing more. Without touching or speaking, I could remain next to him. That wasn't an option. I would be in the medical team's way. Again, I retreated to our assigned room and waited. We may be able to return around four o'clock that afternoon. Time passed slowly with simple distractions - observations and judgments on the childcare center, re-reading hospital literature, creating insignificant to-do lists, feeble attempts at primping, and prayer. Plenty of prayer. I didn't make or accept many telephone calls; only a few calls from the older kids anxious to visit. I had to prepare and disappoint them that a visit with mom and dad was okay but the visit with the new brother would have to wait another day.

While waiting for their arrival, we had our second quick visit with James post-op.

"How is everything?" I inquired to the male nurse, Ray.

"He is doing great! There's a little carbon dioxide retention but nothing we can't work with." At this point, I had no idea what "carbon dioxide retention" implied so I only spoke to the "work with" phrase, "Are you sure?"

"Oh yea," he replied without hesitation.

Ray went on to say the next time I came to visit I could probably feed him. "We will be taking off him the vent very soon." The surgeon's partner, an elderly man with a gray and slightly receding hairline was moving around behind the nurse but clearly looking at and tending to James. As the nurse spoke, I looked to this doctor for some information or clue. He was focused on his work.

I interrupted the nurse. My eyes looked to the man wearing a long white coat when I asked, "Are you sure that's okay? Please don't rush him. So long as he will be okay, I can wait."

"I'm sure," the nurse replied as he looked to the direction of my focus. "Dr. Raphaely is right here and ready."

I was completely ignorant of all of this. I knew my son. That is all. I repeated, "Just don't rush him. I can wait. So long as James will be okay, I can wait to feed him." With that, another kiss, a gentle stroke, and a few sweet nothings whispered, regrettably I walked away again.

It was time to gather composure and focus on three other children. We met them in the cafeteria for dinner. It was great to see them. Even better to see their smiles and excitement. I couldn't eat. Feeling terribly guilty for it, I just couldn't stop worrying. It was such a terrible pull to be there seeing fun and life with these three yet know the other was with strangers and completely unaware of the wonders life had to offer. Without me, how could he possibly know to push through the pain?

Somehow, I managed.

After the kids ate, we enjoyed the beautiful and colorful playground then explored the Child Life Room. More fun to be had. Unfortunately, a sense of immediacy was rising within me. It started quietly and gradually. For a while, I was able to stave it off and discount it as an overly protective, meddling parent neurosis. When would I learn to trust and have faith?

I was unable. I was a complete failure. At exactly, 7:40 PM I looked at the clock on the wall, turned to these visitors and said it was time to go. I needed to be with James immediately. I was reminded we had another twenty minutes to wait.

"Well, let's' start walking the kids out and be ready in the room to call at 8."

It was a rushed and impolite adieu. I couldn't help myself. I felt sick and anxious, like throwing up. This distance between my son and I felt like it was growing far beyond my control.

Once we reached the room on 2B, my husband made the required call to the CICU, "Hi. We are coming down to see our son." After a brief minute or two my husband hung up and shared, "They said we can't right now. They are working on someone." I couldn't focus and felt like my body would just sink. I decided on a quick shower for busy work and perhaps some relief from the anxiety. As I dressed, there was a knock and then muffled voices in the next room.

It was the sudden and serious discussion with the tall stranger that seemed to be speaking Greek despite the English vocabulary. Now, my husband and I were left alone. Stunned. Lost. Confused. Desperate. We were motionless for a moment in this small room as far from the CICU as anyone on the cardiac floor could be. Room 7. Floor 2B. Despite being together, our minds and bodies began to take two divergent paths. I looked at him, he at me. Without a word, he took a chair, placed it in the hallway in front of our room, faced it in the direction of the CICU, sat, crossed his arms, and waited. He'd wait in that position all night. I turned and looked out the window. It was dark now. The children from the childcare center were gone. The sky was crowded with stars. There was an eerie silence on the ward.

While life goes on for the healthy and their healthy children, there is a much different world happening on another dimension called pediatric hospitals. Even in them, a cardiac floor is a world unto itself. Shortly after arriving at the children's hospital, we were greeted warmly by parents whose "heart babies" were a few hours, days, or months in care ahead of our own. They gingerly approached. Though there is an immediate acceptance it isn't with the same openness and excitement as a parent cocktail party or the first neighborhood block party you attend with your child in tow. It is not even the same as the people you meet in the waiting room of a pediatrician's office while getting a well-baby check. These parents know something. They can't hide it as much as they might try. Even though at times they try to hide it from their subconscious.

I noticed this as soon as I arrived and, frankly, was happy to keep my distance. Told again and again that my child was "so healthy" and in fact, "the healthiest child in the CICU." It wasn't my place to fathom what these heart families may be facing or have to face. I was a lucky one. With only one anomaly (which wasn't even located in the heart itself but rather a great vessel) with long-standing successful treatment, my worries should be a fraction of theirs. Nonetheless, I was greeted with sincere warmth and eye contact as they managed just brief hellos.

As the evening wore on and we were all trapped on this ward, our welcome began to wear out. During rounds and other times by choice of physicians no one, not even parents were allowed in the CICU. An "event" was one of those "other times." Therefore, we waited and the rest of the ward was forced to wait with us. Most stayed in their rooms, certainly away from our end of the corridor. As I prayed for my son, they prayed in gratitude. I would have done the same.

Time continued to inch. An hour. Two hours. Eventually all were led out of their rooms by impatience. There were a few babies in the CICU and their moms, dads wanted to check on them too. Everyone was scared. It was staggered and most headed towards the nurse's station for personal updates. One mom, accompanied by the strength of her mother, came to our room and asked, "How are you?" Their son had the same condition as ours, was born a week earlier without the benefit of a prenatal diagnosis. His coarct repair occurred just the day before. His was an emergency. He nearly died. I was hugged. They certainly prayed for us, and our James. We joked about how we would laugh about this in playgroup in another year. We would share our sons' "zipper stories," complain about doctors' appointments, and not feel so alone. It was good to look forward despite our peers looking away.

As the hours passed, memories kept me company.

Calculations began immediately - it had been twenty-one years since dad died. The death had just recently been assimilated. Now this. This new life just couldn't die. I had only held him once. Another twenty years in the isolation of grief was not endurable especially since it would probably last much longer. It would last as long as there was breath to take. Besides, I did not want the role of my uncle or this Greek physician with my son's older sisters and brother. He simply could not die. How could I tell them? What words could I possibly place together that would not cause excruciating pain and confusion? Death was not an option.

A week after celebrating my 12th birthday, I celebrated my dad's last. He was fifty-two and in less than a month would be dead of a massive stroke. His brother held my mom up as she entered the cozy three-bedroom colonial home. Opening the door, they appeared in the well-used living room. Someone turned off the television. My siblings and I stood there. Waiting. Wondering. Watching. Afraid to exhale. Our mom was clearly devastated. Something happened. She began to gasp as she attempted a few words. My uncle quickly assessed the futility and quieted her with gentle but firm strokes. I asked, "Where's Dad?" No response.

Again, I implored, "Where's Dad?"

My uncle looked at me and managed, "Your dad is not coming home."

"Can I go see him?"

The sobs of grief erupted from deep within my mother. There was no more to be discussed despite my attempted, "What happened?" The eyes of my older brother and sister were wide as they glared at me in silence. Their sharp glances spoke clearly - there was nothing more to ask. Wait for it to be offered. In a few days, the obituary may offer answers. The first word next to my dad's publicized name was "Suddenly." The next time I saw him, he was in a casket. That was it. Dad was never coming home.

Dad lived with a strong sense of purpose. Some of these memories from my childhood may not be completely accurate becuase I was young and dad's loss was felt deeply. In his absence, I have been left to imagine how events and people affected him. It was hard for anyone to speak of him once he passed. The work to keep on living was a terribly difficult task that did not leave strength for remembering aloud what was missing.

This night would leave a mark, too.

My dad's faith and devotion came out as I walked my prayer back and forth to the CICU countless times. I would not leave the hospital. I would appreciate the awful troubles other souls struggled with that were surely worse than mine were. The one-month memorial service for 9/11 in the hospital chapel was a perfect opportunity. Composure and respect would be maintained. I would sit at my child's bedside, ask his caretakers how *they* are doing, speak to my older children with a smile and forced enthusiasm, manage to eat a bit each day, express breast milk through a machine without remorse, stay clean and coiffed as if there were no troubles. God would certainly be moved to send a miracle. He would personally touch one of these physicians to know exactly what to do, when to save his life, and deliver the miracle.

Shortly before midnight, we were called to James's bedside. We arrived with no forewarning of James's condition and appearance. As we walked the long hallways, I tried to mentally prepare myself for what I would see. Yet, I had no reference point. The medical providers provided no preparation. Would I be able to hold myself up?

The double doors swung open and there lay my son. Only, I couldn't see him. I saw tubes, machinery, and gapers along the route as I walked past. Nurses, doctors, staff, and visitors saw us and quickly turned away but kept us in focus via peripheral vision. I couldn't have cared less save their selfishness.

James looked like the dead frog I barely got through dissecting in ninth grade biology. His arms were down by his sides. His hands no longer clenched. His legs were flopped with the knees facing opposite directions. His head was propped and facing to the left. His skin was no longer pink. It was a gray, green, hazy sort of yellow color. Instead of being wrapped in tubes and wires like a Christmas tree, he had been tied down in a struggle. He was imprisoned.

The tube that was once in his nose was taped forcefully to his mouth. So His skin was pulled taut unnaturally. His chest had two tubes protruding now. Only they didn't lie flat like the one earlier in the day. These were much less flexible. They stuck straight up and out from the center of his now open chest. The only thing between me and the inside of my son's chest cavity was what looked like a thick, square Saran Wrap patch measuring about two inches. Though the tubing was not colored itself, it was filled with red. My eyes followed the tubing as the Greek - speaking physician mumbled something in the background. The tubing went up and out and hung over the right side of the isolette. It was led into a larger machine that swirled and churned. I heard its hum. It was plugged into the wall less than five feet away.

"So, if we turn this off he will die?"

"Yes. Right now, we are letting him rest his heart. This is like baby bypass."

The doctor was still speaking but my ability to focus and understand had become severely challenged as a result of what had already been said. All I knew was that I had a job to do. Not only to keep my son company, but also to make certain no one tripped over that extension cord.

James was christened at midnight on October 4 - 5, 2001 by a Father John. He was called to the bedside after the nurse asked if we would like a priest. "Well, only for baptism. Nothing else." I ordered. We have no record of this save my memory. I went after these records in the months and years that followed but the church was adamant, "we don't make baptismal certificates in an emergency."

October 5 - 7, 2001

Around 8:30 AM, my husband rose from his guard point and walked over to the two veteran doctors that had emerged from a patient's room - a patient with a much easier treatment plan. Now to see the minutes accumulate and other less serious children be addressed was nearly maddening. The only discussion we had with medical staff was the attending physician the night before who repeated his apology and lack of answers, albeit sincere at the time.

So, there in the hallway was the first confrontation. "What happened?' "What will you do now?" "When will we be able to bring him home?"

Of course, there was very little answer for them to give.

The world-renowned surgeon answered, "a bunch of days."

During the bunch of days family visited. As much as I truly appreciated their presence, any time away from my son's bedside was torturous. All his aunts and uncles finally made it to see him over this weekend. With a bedside limit for visitors, I had to give my place over to another. I tried to be polite and appreciative. I wasn't always capable of performing. I attempted to walk my sisters out of the hospital after their visit. At which time my sister told me all the information she was able to get from the nurse practitioner. The medical team had "lost him" that night. I crumbled to the floor. I didn't know that. No one had used those words. How could they tell her and not me? Why did I not understand this?

The first weekend of October 2001 was a momentous one. The world watched as our nation went to war with Afghanistan in retaliation of the 9/11 attacks. On Sunday, October 7 several air attacks were reported. Despite being isolated and confined to the CICU unit of a Delaware children's hospital, the nation's fear permeated the air. Nurses arrived for their shift and spoke aloud of new terror threats they' d heard on the radio, from a friend, or a concerned teenage child. There was fear that the Interstate would be shut down. The Red Cross started a strongly worded blood drive. There may not be enough blood.

Sunday morning I sat next to James. His life now relied on public utilities and volunteer blood donors I grew terrified of what could happen.

"Is there enough blood for him?" I inquired.

"So far."

"Can I donate? I am B+, too."

"No, as the new mom you can't."

The nurse explained further why that was, but I was unable to grasp anything once she responded in the negative.

More inquiries for explanations of all these threats. Not only could my son not have enough blood for this "baby bypass" machine (ECMO) he was dependent on, I feared my children who were a state away would be in danger or in fear and I not able to get to them. Nothing relaxed or reassured me. Everything scared me.

I sat next to my son as much as my lactating breasts would allow and I prayed and caressed and watched an eagle soar out my son's window. The hymn, "On Eagle's Wings," would play in my ear's memory and my heart would fight it off. This was no time for a funeral procession.

October 8 - 11, 2001

At dawn Monday, James was still alive. He had survived more than three full days attached to a machine that had replaced his body's blood supply at least threefold. Respectfully, I returned to my room for the mandatory doctors rounds and much-anticipated discussion with the surgeon who would be back after the weekend's break.

Again, the CICU doors opened and there was my son's bed. My breath and strength gave way as he was no longer attached to his mechanical companion. Dressed in blue the surgeon moved around his bed. Oh my God. I didn't know if this was good or bad. How could I possibly handle another surprise?

Norwood turned and saw us coming.

Shit.

Norwood grinned.

Thank God. James must still be alive.

"We will keep his chest open just in case," Norwood lectured. "It is a good sign that he has made it off the ECMO." ECMO was the artificial circulatory system for my son that I had not wanted unplugged all weekend.

Breathe. Breeeeeathe. Maintain composure. Encourage James. "Hold on, baby. Just a little bit more. You're doing great!"

Pray.

My mother's rosaries, my grandmother's old prayers, and my absolute awe for James's strength kept me upright. The nurse's chair was a help, too.

On Tuesday, Norwood was full of surprises again. The first visit after morning rounds, James's chest was closed. Another good sign.

On Wednesday as the doctors worked to stabilize and wean him from the ventilator, they became concerned for his brain. James began to shake. It was like the shake that accompanied a newborn's stretch, but the shaking wasn't quelled by the stretch's completion. He kept shaking. I asked to cover him. All these days of James laying on his back with nothing but a diaper. For a bit the staff allowed me to wrap him in a blanket. His body quieted, but not for long. There was a request for a neurological consult and an EKG. Once again, though James was not moved for the procedure I was not allowed to be present. Initial results shared by the nursing staff were that everything looked good. There was no bleeding.

With that news, my husband went home to check in with the older children. After rounds at 8PM, the neurologist, Dr. Bean, knocked on the door of Room 7, Floor 2B. He was a short, somewhat stocky gray haired gentle-faced man.

"I did a full neurological exam on your son at the request of Drs. Raphaely and Norwood."

He stopped and asked if there was anyone else nearby to keep me company. He was noticeably concerned when there was not.

"Well, Mrs. Mannix, clearly your son was neurologically sound and healthy at delivery and thereafter. However, I am very concerned that at some point either during or after surgery your son suffered severe insult to his brainstem and his cortex."

Though this doctor didn't even have an accent, I was schooled in child development, and I had not taken any painkillers since I was expressing milk for the baby all I heard was something foreign. It was too much.

I asked, "Will he crawl?"

Dr. Bean tried again, "I am sorry, but I am seriously concerned about your child's ability to meet more than minimal life functions."

He expressed concern about the amount of pharmaceuticals being used on James. The following day his plan would be to examine James again after he had was him off some of the drugs.

He left.

I was pissed. I made the obligatory call to the CICU that I wanted to see my son. Only this time, I did not ask, merely informed, "I am coming to see my son." The phone slammed as it hit the receiver.

I ran.

I ran past the other parents, past the nurse's station, through the corridors and four corners, through the double doors. I only stopped to wash my hands. I would not take any unnecessary risks with this baby's life. I just wasn't so sure if I would be pulling wires off him and bringing him home or not.

His nurse that night was the same one that had accompanied Dr. Kochilas the night James had suffered the "event." Though I never raised my voice because there were young lives resting all around me, the nurse was surprised by my forceful conversation and presence. In no time she disappeared and that night's attending doctor pulled a chair up next to James's bed. I cried as I shared my wishes and fears.

There wasn't much he could say or do. Just protect his nurse, I guess.

The best defense in the institution's arsenal was my own breast milk. Each time I was settled in for the long haul to sit with James, the breast milk would be screaming for release. With no choice, I would leave under forced composure. While expressing, I began my mental list of what research I should do for this next step in James's battle for life – neurology. I was right here in the hospital. Tomorrow I would give the department a visit.

Back in the sterile room our belongings had begun to accumulate. A few baskets of fruit and flowers had arrived. My husband had managed to bring a few comforts from home. There was a small metal crib on one side of the room. Inside it awaited a blue musical teddy bear. I sat on the bed's edge as I perfected the art of mechanically expressing milk despite the constant fear of someone walking in on me. With no locks on the doors and the loud hum of the machine even these fears materialized a couple times. Religiously and carefully, the milk was stored in plastic bags, tapped, and marked with name, date, and time of day. After cleaning up, I would prepare for another visit with James. The refrigerator was on the way. His milk was beginning to overrun the freezer. One nurse asked us to store some of it at home. There was only one freezer and more than one mom storing breast milk. There was just one mom whose baby wasn't getting any though. Dutifully, my husband was sent home with a small cooler full of labeled breast milk.

On Thursday, James was improving. Dr. Murdison remarked on the measurable difference in James's evaluation as compared to the day before. The social worker called to the room requesting breast milk. James could have some of my breast milk through a GI tube.

I collapsed in relief. Finally, measurable progress. Survival was in sight. He could have some of this breast milk. He would have what he was born to enjoy. His body could begin to recover with the help of something not foreign. As I fell like an accordion, dropping to the floor, tears overflowed. We had survived the worst. This was only going to get better from here. In just a few moments, I had gathered myself, my best choice for breast milk, a renewed faith, a lighter step and an encouraging smile accompanied me to the CICU. I passed the breast milk over to the social worker. We all stood and watched as the nurse gently and intermittently injected the milk through the tube. He accepted the nourishment with ease.

My shoulders fell three inches while my stature grew. How proud I was of my trooper. This was news to share. The kids, aunts, uncles, grandparents and co-workers were all updated. James is getting better.

A few hours later and exactly a week from the initial terrifying "crash," we were calmly told by a new attending physician, Dr. Murdison, that James had a pin-size hole in his lung. Initially, the attempt to relieve it was made by reinserting a chest tube. Didn't work. They tried a larger one. Didn't work. The physician was almost serene. He was not alarmed. Yet, he was showing us X-rays. My concern was the amount of radiation the week-old child was being exposed to which was probably the only thing I was able to understand.

It was 4 AM and I sat with James. He was calm and beautiful lying in his isolette.

The nurses came over to withdraw extra fluid from his ventilator tubing. They had to keep doing it. The doctor came over. He began to help. It was quiet but active. I slowly backed away to allow the medical professionals room to do what they needed. Gently I got the attention of a nurse and instructed her, "I have to go express. Please call me or get me if anything happens."

"Of course," she replied.

October 12, 2001

While expressing, I fell asleep. Shortly before 6:30 AM
my husband woke me. He was off to "Parents Day" at our
eldest child's school. Since there had been no call or report in
over two hours from the medical team, it seemed safe for him
to leave. With rounds coming up in less than half an hour, I
put my head on the pillow knowing the souls in Purgatory
would wake me at 7 to be with James.

I closed my eyes.

Back home, I was on our small front lawn. James was
about three and we were having a catch with a large blue ball.
Without a word, he sat down. Then he laid down curled into
the fetal position. I stared for a moment. My feet would not
move. I walked over and knew he was gone. He looked so
peaceful and comfortable. I gently moved him closer to the
flower bed and sat with him. His hand was getting cold. I knew
it was time to tell his dad. How I hated to do this. I would have
to wake my husband to tell him "James is dead."

My eyes opened quickly to the sound of loud
knocking on the door.

But I didn't move. I had learned what comes after the
knock on a hospital room door. I already knew what I would
be told. There were medical professionals at my door and I had
just dreamed that my son had died.

They banged again and called my name. The door
began to open.

I rose to greet them. It was the social worker and the attending physician, Dr. Murdison.

Speaking first, I half questioned and half claimed, "This is it, isn't it?" fully expecting to hear James hadn't made it. Alas, I heard a different combination of words.

"James had a rough couple hours. Dr. Norwood has taken him emergently to the OR which is why he is not here himself to tell you," Dr. Murdison informed me. This was an odd development that left guilt in my stomach. The flow was unnatural. Years later while searching for understanding as to what happened, I found there were physicians who may have considered a different, more collaborative, approach to death and dying.

Dr. Nuland, a surgeon and author, watched his mother, grandmother and aunt die as a relatively young man. He entered the medical field hoping to be what his family physician was to his Bronx family. A steady support that allowed for the patient's input in his/her own care. As time passed and rapid beneficial discoveries were made in the medical field, he like so many other professionals gained a confidence that would be his nemesis and starkest challenge. When his own brother was diagnosed with an aggressive cancer, instead of speaking honestly of the poor prognosis Dr. Nuland denied his brother the knowledge. Dr. Nuland, with the dangerous combination of medical knowledge and cockiness combined with the devotion of a brother, unwittingly made decisions that would affect his brother's death. Calling in favors and friends, Dr. Nuland secured trial medications for his brother. It led to more suffering and, of course, eventual death. He acknowledges in "How We Die," "With this burden on my shoulders, I made mistakes."

"Physicians misunderstand the ingredients of hope, thinking it refers only to cure or remission." Dr. Nuland recognizes the spirituality that physicians can take away from their patients and families. There are few physicians that would argue against the strong relationship between mind and body. Cardiologists from the early twentieth century, Dr. Levine instructed Dr. Lown to give optimism to the patient and leave the pessimism to himself. However, these cardiologists of two generations ago perhaps because death was not so easily fought by technology, were able to acknowledge when death had won.

Dr. Nuland writes, "Medicine's humility in the face of nature's power has been lost, and with it has gone some of the moral authority of times past."

The control over a loved one's death is to be given to the family by birthright.

I would have liked a Dr. Nuland during that second week of October.

"Where is your husband?" the social worker asked.

I remembered he was in rush hour on a major highway. He would have to come back.

"Yes. Call him and we will let you know how it goes."

"Please get me as soon as I can be with him!" I pleaded.

My prayer started with an Act of Contrition as it appeared I had prematurely given up. James was still fighting, and so would I.

Hours passed again. Just as slow as any other day and any other procedure. At 10:00, the phone rang. James was in CICU, and we could come down. We marched with a quick pace, absent any preparation or idea of what awaited us. The double doors opened. All I could see at James's bed was blue. It was a parade of blue crowding the main event. The blue scrubs melted away the closer we came to center stage.

In a soft whisper my body released, "Oh."

"Oh, no."

I stood there as shock crept up like the wave of a gentle sea to insulate my soul. I was suddenly lifeless. Immobile. It had been ten days of fruitlessly trying to hold back tears. There was nothing in this CICU that didn't seem like a child's drawing smudged by water. But not now. My eyes were dry. Why hadn't anyone the courage to prepare us? Just hours before, he was a pink and rosy baby. Now he was covered in purple and black and blue. He was bleeding from an open wound on his right side. Somebody made a feeble attempt to cover it with a blanket. His right hand, though clenched again, was perfectly black. He was swollen. His size was that of one of my children at nine months, not ten days. His eyes were so badly swollen he couldn't have opened them even if he had wanted to. The tubes were all back. There were even more than before. The machines were back.

This time, the milkshake tubes came out of his right side. His mouth was no longer taped so severely but his nose was. And there was noticeable bruising (black where the rest of his face was a reddish purple) where the tape was once so forcefully placed. I knew he was already gone. These damn machines could bring a year cold corpse back to life to torture family members. Whereas nine days ago the unexpected wires were hopeful, now, they were the chains that bound a tethered soul.

And I now knew why I had never seen my father again. Some things are not meant for a child's eyes. Others are not meant for a mother's.

The social worker pulled us away to introduce a thickly accented gray-haired young man. He had helped Norwood with the surgery. As he began to explain what had happened and what had been done to our son, Michael focused on one question, "Where is Norwood?"

"He is not here right now."

"He performed this surgery?"

"Yes."

"Well, where is he?"

"Well, he has left this doctor here to help you," the social worker offered.

"But when did you finish?"

"Just now."

"Then where is Norwood?"

"He is busy."

This was absolutely unacceptable and firmly told to the staff. We needed to speak with the man making decisions in our son's medical care immediately.

We reluctantly headed back to not-so-lucky Room 7 to wait for Norwood. He was as stunned as we were when we crossed paths in the hallway. He tried to escape by walking around me. I stepped in front of him but was unable to speak. Michael did.

"Norwood?"

"Oh," he fumbled. "Did you speak with my associate?"

"Yes. But we need to speak with you?"

"He could help you."

My husband knew to re-direct. "What is the treatment plan now?"

"What do you mean?"

"Well, James is back on ECMO. What now?"

"He will remain on that over the weekend."

"And you will be around this weekend?"

"Oh no. I will not."

"Well who will be overseeing James's care, then?" my husband asked.

"I don't know."

"What do you mean?"

"I don't know who will be on this weekend."

"Don't you oversee this operation?"

"Yes, but scheduling is not up to me," he offered weakly.

"Well, could you tell me who will be overseeing James's care this weekend?"

"What difference does knowing that make now?" the world-renowned-has-a-procedure-named-after-him -surgeon stated more than asked.

That woke me from the survival-instinct stupor that shock begets. "What!" I must have yelled for the feeling was intense. I had never and have never felt more of the innate mother instinct to protect my child than I did at that moment. My mouth flapped with threats and questions as much as I tried hard to remain composed.

"This is MY child. You can't get away with this. I may just be a preschool teacher but you can't treat a baby like this, let alone my baby!"

My husband stepped between us. I noticed unlike all his staff, Norwood was dressed in plain clothes - absent any lab coat or ID tag. White shirt, dark pants, and a red tie with pictures of young children all over it. I wondered what I was saying. What could I do? What were my instincts telling me? He wasn't telling me something. It was palpable.

My intent in my rampage was not to set up a lawsuit. My intent was to scare the doctor into allowing me to have some control of my son's life again and my family's destiny. After seeing his condition just moments previous, I knew my son would not survive. He had actually already died but had been left in this torturous no-man's land. I knew he would have to let go. The drama I was centered in forbade me from clear and productive thought processes. In hindsight, I know I was looking for professional guidance for what I as a layperson already knew was happening but had never handled previously. How would turning off the machines work? How long would he have to remain in that tangle of wires, and that pre-decomposing-state, and in front of all the other patients, families, visitors, medical providers? I wasn't embarrassed. Rather, my family's privacy was being encroached upon. I was never a mother for a videotaped birth. Though I certainly had never thought about it before, I did not want gawkers at my baby's death, either. There is an immoral trespass on families whose loved one's death is caught on tape or in the public eye. Death is not a circus freak show yet here it was and my James was in the center ring.

I was firmly restrained as my husband strongly and respectfully again implored, "Can you please let us know who will be overseeing James's care this weekend?"

"Yes. I will let you know."

We let him pass and his relief showed as the left corner of his mouth curled up.

My husband's brother and sisters availed themselves. Michael stayed close to them as he tried to understand where we were and what was happening. I really didn't seek nor want company that day. I felt quite certain of what had happened. It was a struggle to see James suffering in the condition he was in. I stood over his bed alone as my husband spent time with his family. I knew James was in the meaningful ways already gone. Any moments now were on borrowed time. These were his gift to us. He was in too much pain for him to stay of his own want or desires. Michael needed to come to this conclusion on his own.

I stood by James's bedside afraid to touch him. Afraid to ask to see his open wound. The nurse was one we'd never had before. She was methodical and detached. Very little eye contact was made. She didn't look at my son. Her focus was on the medications and the chart. Click. Slam. Click click. The equipment made more noise tonight than any other previous evening.

"There is still some blood on his forehead," I mentioned to the nurse.

Without word, she brought over a small tub of water, washcloth, and Johnson's baby bath. "You can give him a bath," she instructed.

"Oh, okay."

It was his only one.

I wiped the blood from his brow and arms. Gently I moved down his legs and maneuvered around where the blanket disguised his bleeding wound. He had become even larger since the morning. He looked to be in so much pain.

"James, I am so sorry," I confessed.

"I will miss your need of me and your deep soulful eyes and your voice, your cries and whatever your laugh would have sounded like. James, I will miss the slow Mommy and Baby dances we will never have. But James, you will always have me. I will only ever be a thought away."

So tiny being just 10 days old. I didn't know the rituals in an ICU could become similar to that on death row.

The small goldenrod dishpan filled with bubbles and tepid water helped soak the plain white, antiseptic cloth. Ever so gently, I wiped his brow. Discolored. Purple and blue. Memory did not forsake me I was sure. This child was born with a healthy pink glow. That his color and size could change so grossly in ten days was cruel. Red came up onto the washcloth. I wiped around his head without moving him. So afraid to do more harm than good. Wiped around his eyes. They were swollen. I still didn't want to sting them with soap. He still had the shape of his dad's brows. And his sister's. A tear escaped from the corner of his eye and rolled down his oversized, discolored cheek.

"Oh, look!" I called the attention of his nurse. "He is crying."

"That is the fluid trying to get out wherever it can," she stated like an inanimate computer-driven robot.

That made me cry.

Closely my lips spoke in my sweet baby's ears, "Mommy's here, honey. Mommy knows. Mommy is so sorry. I am going to miss you, too." Then bits of the James Taylor tune I had been trying to remember all week began ringing in my ears:
"…and ten thousand miles behind me and ten thousand more to go….

…..a song that they sing in the sky……….

So good night all you moonlight ladies..

Rock a bye sweet baby James"

.......deep breath. I needed more time. This couldn't
be all.

I kissed him and cried. Three more tears flowed from
his eyes. With extreme care, I wiped each one.

This was my baby and I just hanging out on a Friday
night with everyone else gone. Bathtime. I wish he could have
nursed. The washcloth made its way down his left arm. Gentle.
Be so careful. I was unable to get the discoloration off, but at
least, he was clean. Oh what a shoulder he had. It was still
fuzzy.

I tried the right shoulder but stumble over all the lines.
I can't. I just can't look under the blanket draped over his right
side. There was an open incision there from surgery this
morning. And his hand. His right hand was so purple it
appeared black. Helpless. Useless, failing mother. His belly.
Yes, his belly. Distended and swollen, yet still fresh and new.

His feet – so precious. Just a day before socks were on
his toes. A wipe of the bottom of his feet though they never
touched the ground. Scrub gently between his toes. Dry them
off with a soft receiving blanket. Kiss. Kiss the bottom of this
baby's feet with delight and anxiety, fear and pride. This was
MY son.

Click. Snap. Beep. Click.

The nurse's job brings me back. Medications being
administered. Monitors being checked. Lines and tubes
adjusted. Seems rough. Very callous. The medical staff has
removed themselves. No longer are we receiving the jovial

welcomes and discussions volunteered with open arms. No gentle support. They no longer look at my son close enough to see his features. He is no longer a baby. He has become a case. Doctors, and perhaps by extension all medical providers, forget there is more to heal after a patient can no longer be saved. Describing the scene so often found in hospitals after a rescue attempt fails, there is a quick distancing by the failed rescuers.

"…..the room is strewn with the debris of the lost campaign. In the center of the devastation lies a corpse and it has lost all interest for those who, moments earlier were straining to be the deliverers of the man whose spirit occupied it."(Nuland)

Though the machines still beeped, one doing the job of his heart another his lungs, my son's spirit had already left the body of this patient. It was a battle lost and a number that they would prefer to forget. I was now "the family" for the funeral director to handle. For their sanity, my title of "Mom" had been replaced by the more formal – "Mrs."

Without asking, the nurse took the dishpan away. The towel placed in the medical waste receptacle. I was silently pointed to a chair if I had to stay. I was no longer welcome. I sat clutching the small, nearly full bottle of baby bath. I stared. My son. It was so awful to see him that way. My heart ached. My breasts hurt. I would come back. I was so scared that I would not.

I gave my son a bath. His last.

My husband appeared with Dr. Bhat, the doctor that did the initial prenatal diagnosis.

It was time for a very private consultation. As never before, the doctor led us into an office behind the cath lab and around the corner from the CICU. He seemed to be anticipating something loud or disturbing.

Once we all were sitting, Michael posed the million-dollar question, "what happened? You were with us in the summer. You said, no open heart, nothing to worry about. What happened?"

And again, "What happened?"

The cardiologist looked down at the floor. He would be among the first of many that would struggle to not only answer our questions but to meet our gaze. Eventually he managed a reply. It was just three words: "You trusted us."

He repeated himself, "You trusted us."

"Nature's first green is gold,

Her hardest hue to hold.

Her early leaf's a flower;

But only so an hour.

Then leaf subsides to leaf.

So, Eden sank to grief,

So, dawn goes down to day.

Nothing gold can stay."

~ Robert Frost

October 13, 2001

Few can describe what it is like to hold a dead baby. There are few that have had the experience. Yet, more than most would like to imagine. Holding a life lost that has just begun. Looking at the face of birth, touching skin that is fresh and new, to caress fingers that have only touched you and know that all hope is dead. At 8:00 on an autumn Saturday, machines were turned off. James was unable to make his heart beat again on his own. He was unable to move air though his lungs. The organs that for nine months I had worked to bring to a maturity enough to survive without my assistance had the lost the power they were born with. The soul that had arrived just eleven days prior had lost a body to house it. His body could not be put back in me. However I became a lifetime host of his soul. I do not know exactly when he died. I accompanied him in his process of dying, but was kept away when the moment came. I knew we would now miss out on birthday celebrations, graduations, weddings, and more. Here I was kept away from his moment of death. Parents enjoy dying first because without a doubt you will be there in spirit at their death. Trapped in mortality however, those whose children die first often lose that unique and most beautiful of bonds. How I wish I could have mimicked the words from" Steel Magnolias:" "I was here when [he] came into the world and I was there when [he] left." I wasn't. A machine was his final companion.

A dead baby is heavy. The weight belies the size. Mine was heavier than most, for certain. The procedures and surgeries and mechanisms that were put upon his tiny frame left a body tortured, misshapen, discolored, and swollen. His eyes were so severely swollen shut his race could be questioned in death. Despite being under the light of a warmer and finally swaddled as a baby should, he was cold. His lips, blue and black were too large and left an icy sting when I kissed them. A curtain was pulled for the first time around bed #5. I sat in the hard maple rocking chair struggling to not look away from my baby. I wanted to deny him in death. He was such a beautiful baby. He had been just as perfect as his older brother and sisters had been in infancy. How could I be so callous as to look away? I held him. I passed him to his dad. I quickly took him back. He was so heavy. He was so cold. He was so tightly bound in hospital blankets all I could see was his face. Purple, black, deep red. His new baby smell was gone. Who would help me? I didn't know what to do. No one was there. No one would hold me. I will never recall what helped me stand up, place him back in the hospital's bed then walk away. There was no social worker. There was no nurse. There was no physician. I walked the endless hallway and made my way back to the living children. I left James and his milk at DuPont. A funeral home was directed to take care of him from there. James's feet never touched the ground. He would be carried from me to a nurse to a doctor to a transport team to a nurse to a doctor to a surgeoun to a nurse to a funeral director. If any forgot carrying James when he was alive, all of us who held him in death remember. Heavy.

The first two weeks of October surely passed quickly for many that year. The nation's attention was focused on New York City, the Pentagon, a field in Pennsylvania and in Afghanistan. There was ire that our country did not offensively react quickly enough after the attacks of a month ago. Yet, for those parents watching a sick child fight against the strength of many with advanced medical degrees, a lifetime passed. I was by my son's side every moment that I wasn't preserving breast milk or following the doctor's visiting hour protocols. There is still regret. The most regret is surrounding the lost opportunity to be with James when he was being refused oxygen.

The ride home was under a crisp, blue mid-Autumn sky. Everything in the world looked clear. Bright. Beautiful. On an October Saturday morning, the traffic was light on Interstate 95. The three lanes of traffic heading north from Delaware were uncrowded, allowing motorists their first choice of speeds. For those rushing to their next destination, the passing lane was clear. For those going about their scheduled business in a timely manner, the middle lane provided a place to move at their preferred speed. Leaving the right and left space on either side of the vehicle an option around whatever may
fall in their way. It was the most occupied lane that morning. The far right lane is available. Of course, that is the slow lane for the elderly drivers who have witnessed enough tragedy in their long lives already. No need to risk more. Who travels Interstate 95 on a Saturday morning at 55 miles per hour? There was no one in that lane except our white van. Others zoom past at all speeds. No matter how fast or slow their motors were running, our van could have been standing still. The eagle soaring and circling above even moved at a quicker clip. Where was everyone rushing? How odd. They don't seem to know what just happened to the two parents inside this slow-moving vehicle. We didn't know either. I am sure we

looked like any other young couple heading to complete chores or watch a soccer game. We already had all the equipment for those roles. The minivan, of course. Odds and ends of different sports in the hatch - a hockey stick, some baseballs, even a swim bag. Three different schools were advertised on the rear windshield. Me in a baseball cap and exercise pants. The driver, my husband, was in a baseball cap and blue jeans. The booster sat in the middle seat behind the driver. The new baby car seat was in the middle seat behind the passenger. The radio was silent. There was no discussion. There were no children interrupting any adult conversation.

No one would expect to see or understand the mountain of bags, blankets, and pillowcases that were hiding all the normal minivan accoutrements. Inside were the odds and ends that parents of very sick children acquire while "living" in the hospital. These are the insignificant things that accompany you while waiting for some doctor, nurse, surgeon, or administrator to say, "You can bring him home." There are the clothes brought by in-laws from home. There is the comforter from the master bedroom to make you feel more like sleeping in the sterile environment that your child MUST remain in. There are baskets of fruit, flowers and goodies delivered from co-workers hoping your return from work will not be pre-empted by an untimely funeral. The clothes so thoughtfully selected as your new arrival's "Coming home Outfit" with all the store tags still attached in the overnight bag. We can live without all these things we are towing. How are we supposed to live leaving our son behind? Instead of nursing my Wawa cappuccino and his Diet Coke, we each hold blank stares and I a little green box.

I cradle the box firmly but gently in my tired arms. It is a little bigger than a textbook but nowhere near as heavy. It feels smooth and strangely comforting. It gives my useless arms something to do. It reminds me of wool blankets with silk edging. I used to gently rub the silk next to my skin as a young girl. Those gentle cheek rubs of the "silky" blanket would give me either soothing comfort or a fun, little, skin tickle that made me smile. Oddly enough, there is a baby blanket waiting at home the same color as this box, mint green, with an edging of the softest silk. The green blanket had comforted my 4 year old daughter, Grace, since she was a born. Her older brother had shared it with her upon her arrival to our family. And his older sister shared it with him when he came home from the hospital. Grace was now anxious to share it with her new baby brother.

I hugged the box. I stroked the box. I stared at the box. I looked at my baby's
father. He drives. He keeps his eyes on the road. My mind needs to stay with the box. My grip loosens so the box can rest on my lap. The box is held closed with a small matching green ribbon tied in a perfect bow. Why did I get a green box? I had a baby boy. Why isn't the box blue? He was a baby boy. If I open the box now will I be able to make the bow perfect again when I am finished? Is it worth the risk? But is there something of my son in the box? I need to see my son. I need to be with my son.

As I gingerly undo the bow, I realize this box will open down the middle. Right down the center. I will have to open it like the surgeon opened my son's chest. I will be careful. I will pull open each side and remember that what is inside is sacred. It is an honor to see the inside. No one should ever have to expose their heart to a stranger. And yet the newborn little boy did. He paid with his life and he left my heart exposed to the world for the rest of mine.

As I opened the box no tears formed in the corners of my eyes. Instead, anger began to fill from every pore. A picture was taken of my martyr after his demise. A request I could not have made clearer to the nurse who asked. "No. Oh, no. I do NOT want a picture of him like that." Worse yet, there was no warning that it had been placed there. I had just had to hold my dead baby in that condition. It was hard to look at him. He still

looked like he was in pain. He still looked like he had been butchered for absolutely no reason. The last day of his life he could not open his eyes because they were so badly swollen. His coloring had been perfect. Within a five hour time span, he had gone from a beautiful little Caucasian boy with his dad's features and my round face to a grotesquely

distorted purple, blue, and black extra large baby I didn't recognize save the soft dusting of hair. And his light colored eyebrows. He would have been my blond-haired child. I never wanted to see a photo of him like that. That was an image I already knew I would have difficulty forgetting. It is an image that could make me take my own life. Yet, here

it is. The pretty mint green box holds a picture of my son after death.

Quickly, I shut those little green doors and the bow fell.

I rested my elbow on the car door and my chin in my hand. I kept one hand on

this new important box in my life. I tried to see my son

somewhere up in that grand sky. The eagle was still soaring overhead. Again, I heard the hymn. That is a song that should be sung at the funeral. It should have been played at his wedding instead. I glimpsed into my future. Only one daughter-in-law. Missing grandchildren. Construction paper Mother's Day cards that I will never receive. One less team for my husband to coach in Little League. I have to tell his brother and sisters. Good god. The pain this will create.

I looked down to reassure myself that the gifts for the older three are with us and weren't misplaced in packing up the van. After holding my son's lifeless body and running into one of his doctors in the hallways, we stopped in the hospital Gift Shop. We weren't bringing home their much anticipated baby brother. I had to bring home something. I knew we could get a charm for his two big sisters' charm bracelets. That is always a nice keepsake, remembrance of a special event. Was this event something to remember? It was more difficult deciding on an item for his 9-year-old big brother. Something that he could remember him by. Something that wouldn't get played with or ruined, but something that would be appreciated. For lack of something better, I settled on a purple angel bear with the word "Peace" stitched in his paw. Peace would be hard to come by now.

It was strange to make these purchases while acting in a socially acceptable
manner. I asked the cashier for some ribbon or something. She gave it to me. Why didn't I just ask her to tie the bows? My hands were shaking. My heart pounding. My mind wanted to scream. My husband staying close, feeling just as lost and alone and terrified as I. Yet, the gift packages looked pretty - giving

no clue as to the pain endured in their fruition. Would these little trinkets help ease anything? Probably not.

We have gotten farther. I don't know what to expect when I get home. We have not given anyone forewarning of our arrival. It was a decision Michael and I made mutually without discussion. Perhaps we were just too terrified to put the words together in a complete sentence. Let alone, say them aloud to another person. That would just make the tragedy more real. Regardless, we couldn't avoid them for much longer. As long and endless as the drive seemed, we were getting closer to home.

With three older children, a sister-in law and aunt at home, and plenty of family and friends in the immediate area....this quiet solitude was going to come to an end quickly. If I was going to see what was in this box without interruption, then I would have to look soon. Another glance at my dear broken husband. His eyes still fixed forward. Still driving. How is he doing it? I was so grateful for him in that moment.

Back to the box.

With a deep breath that I held, I opened the box again. This time I only opened the right side flap. On the inside of this flap was a black ink footprint that belonged to James. Is it the right size? Was his foot as swollen as the rest of his body when they took this print? Was I already forgetting? I kissed that foot so many times. But not nearly as much as I could if he was still here. Would I really never kiss that foot again? My Uncle Joe used to
tell the story of why he had so many children – baby feet. He told me at a family barbecue after my first child was born, "As soon as their fat feet started to flatten out, I would tell my wife

'Time for another.' I just love when they are babies." I wonder what he would do if any of his babies' feet never flattened out. What to plan for now?

What would I do now?

There was a small white envelope. I hoped it would reveal some clue as to how to act and react to this new life. I opened it realizing it must be from the medical staff. Yes it is. The print on the card is that sickening mint green color again. They must have had to invest in these boxes for moms of daughters too. They never know if they will be listing a female or a male as an unsuccessful surgery. Green was a safe color. I wonder how many other unlucky families have one of these. How many does the hospital buy to "have on hand?"

This first sympathy card was generic. Worse yet, there was only one signature - "The Cardiac Center Staff." They didn't sign it individually. There were no personal condolences. No mention of how much James meant to them. No mention of how incredibly beautiful of a baby he was. How sweet. How unique. How special. How much he would be missed. Maybe they would do that individually later, perhaps by sending at least one representative to the funeral. They were James's extended family. They knew him better than his aunts and uncles. Even better than his sisters and brother.

Oh, should I show them this box? How was I to tell them that their baby brother died? This was just so sad. There were no words for the depth of sadness this reaches.

Strange. An unused baby cap and matching new baby hospital gown were also in
this pretty, useless box. Why are they there? My son never wore them? This gouged at my insides even more. All that he

never wore, never touched, never tasted (what would I do with the frozen breast milk?), never felt, never smelled, never saw. His body would be buried in a few days and I would never hold him again. Shivers flew down my spine. NO!

I closed the box again and almost threw it on the dash. I shook my head and hugged my body. I reached into my pocket for James's socks. This is what he did wear. He had an occasional diaper on during his 11 day life. Never anything else except for these socks. The day that we thought he was showing rapid improvement I was allowed to put these plain, white, cotton Baby Gap socks on his tender toes and feet. It will always be remembered as one of my life's greatest moments. Simply putting socks on my newborn's feet. How many mom's out there DON'T take the time to keep the constantly kicked off socks on their child's chubby little feet? Blessings often look more like daily little annoyances. I would always keep those socks with me.

Ten minutes down the road from home and there was more in that box. Information about support groups. The Compassionate Friends. UNITE.

Ugh!

Underneath everything at the bottom of the box was something I would not normally have saved until maybe his first birthday. In a clear plastic medical specimen bag is a clipping of my son's hair. The tears started. Just a few. God forbid, I let many flow, I may never have recovered to help my older children bear this news. I reached carefully into the bag. The contents are precious, priceless, unique. My index finger touched the soft, down-like wisps of hair. I felt a warm wave envelop me from my heart to my empty yet still distended

womb. I close my eyes and quietly whispered, "James."

October 17, 2001

Lying in an unknown place, my head being stroked by an unfamiliar hand, confidence and compassion were being delivered to me. My eyes remained closed as I slowly came out of a pharmaceutically induced midday rest. The surrounding noises were not foreign at all. Driven footsteps of plastic clogs on clean linoleum passing, muffled voices discussing lasix, blood gases, and family supports were creeping through the paper thin barriers. There were rhythmic sounds of mechanical beeps, alarms, and keyboard taps; distinct smell of germicide and sickness wafted by my bed in unwelcome unison. These warm strokes were reassuring. I didn't know where I was, how I got there, or who could possibly be making me feel as reassured as receiving your mother's loving embrace.

Oh.

Oh no.

A mother's loving embrace. Immediately my arms remembered. Their dead weight screamed from either side of my heart. The remainder of my body recalled the events of the previous two weeks as well. A discomfort enrobed me as I writhed from within. The stroking was replaced with two careful and strong arms pushing me back against the white sterile pillow. I shook my head so the nurse couldn't stroke. How could I be comforted? What right did I have as a failed mother have to feel one ounce of comfort when my newborn was lying in a box in the ground?

It is a relief when you awake from a nightmare. I was having this crazy reversal of fortune. I wasn't waking up. As often as I went to sleep in the hopes that I could wake from this nightmare, each and every rest ended with me back in the unthinkable.

Perhaps an aid was added to my IV. Perhaps I just gave in for a few moments. Regardless, the nurse was eventually successful in keeping me still. I had little left to fight anyway. As she gently stroked my head, I confessed, "I buried my son today." My eyes looked up to see her reflect back a sense of pity and helplessness. It was the first of many. For a person much more comfortable giving and helping than taking and being a recipient, I had to look away. There I caught sight of an orange band unknowingly secured around my wrist clearly marked with capital letters in permanent ink - "NUTS." Hmmm. They know. There can be no sanity now

Imagery certainly helps in the successful realization of an event. I imagined my children's birthdays, first days of school, holidays, weddings and other less memorable life events I had never imagined my child's funeral. I had absolutely no idea how to do this. I had done the unthinkable funeral before when my father died and I was just a child myself. As a child the pressure was off. I literally leaned on adults. My uncle held me up as I processed behind my father's casket. This was an alien experience. My own children would be looking to me in addition to the myriad of well-meaning gawkers that want to see how I live with the "unimaginable, incomprehensible, and unfair."

I decided on the "Jackie O" route. Dignified and reserved. No tears would be shed during the funeral. I would not speak to other mourners. I would go in, get this done and leave. I would keep the balance of my children intact. I chose the yellow dress. Just like the summery dress I wore at dad's funeral. I did not allow my children to wear black.

I wanted to ask to see James before they closed the casket. Afraid that would be doing the wrong thing I stayed silent and waited for questions and cues from my husband, the priest and the funeral director. Seeing James was never mentioned. It felt morbid and shameful to need this kind of confirmation. So, James was buried. I never saw him again after I walked away from the CICU three days prior. This ill-thought decision would be highly regrettable as scandals in the funeral home and cemetery businesses surfaced within the following years. It raised the question of whether my son was actually buried in the plot. Or did someone take his body in full or in part to utilize for science or study or some other purpose?

I called the funeral home at least twice after he died to ask if they remembered him and his condition upon arrival. I asked who dressed him and if there was any difficulty getting him dressed for burial. When the answer was yes it offered some reassurance for a little while. I carefully selected a newborn size nightgown for his peaceful rest.

I searched the communion line for members of his medical team. I saw cousins from out of town, my students' parents, my children's classmates and teachers. I saw aunts and uncles I hadn't seen in years. I saw a couple nieces and nephews. But, no one from the hospital. Crazy to have thought it possible but I missed them already. Bonds were formed. At least for me. Their time and investment was appreciated and I wanted to tell them so. Alas, it would have to wait.

My four year old daughter, Grace, leaned over and asked if the baby was all cut up in the casket. Dear. What her young mind was unable to understand was going to be challenging for some time.

My sister couldn't finish her reading. She kept crying. I kept saying in my head, "Come on. You can do it. Let people hear this reading. It is all James gets." There was no reception line. I followed the casket out the door, to the hearse, and got in our minivan parked behind it. I put my head down and cursed the mourners not following my cues. They hung around outside of the church. I sat there hoping they'd all just get in their cars so we could leave. A few came to my window offering gentle and sincere condolences. How awkward. I felt dreadful for being so unwelcoming and unkind in my thoughts. It was all so wrong and I was so bad. These were good people. Their children were alive.

When we reached the cemetery I waited again for the other mourners to quiet the chatter and gather around the 36 inch casket. The smallest most of us had ever seen. The October wind was fierce. So, instead of laying the white rose on top of the coffin I put it in the handle to ensure it would stay. Then I stood there watching everyone else do the same. My uncle, the oldest in his family, the only physician in the family, and father to ten children told me graveside: "All these births and all these years. This is the first one to die."

Eventually we made it home and the festivities began. Kids were running around the house. My sisters and mother were putting out food I didn't know was available. Relatives were catching up with one another. I admired the cake - "God Bless James Matthew." He was here. If not in flesh, in word. James Matthew. It was a great name too. I wasn't sure I even wanted it served. Perhaps I would just freeze it. Proof that he did exist and I wasn't crazy.

It probably was not surprising that a visit to a hospital was part of that day. It wasn't until arriving from the emergency room I was reminded that I had an allergic reaction to the pine nuts in a pignoli cookie. The one item I managed to eat that day. Though stressful it did relieve some pain for a few moments. Only to be replaced later when the cake was gone. All the well-meaning souls had cut and divvied it up for guests. I was heartbroken. I was so stupidly, selfishly heartbroken that his name was gone. Stressful situations can heighten an allergic reaction. Since childhood, my throat would give an awkward tingle and tightness after eating certain nuts. Never a truly alarming reaction - more of annoyance. On this day, my son's funeral and the day before my tenth wedding anniversary, I had one bite and my throat itched like I had swallowed poison ivy. Heat rose from my throat radiating to my whole head and extremities. Not wanting to cause a reason for any more drama than was already present at the funeral reception of an eleven-day-old, I quietly disappeared to the upstairs bathroom in search of Benadryl. I drank from the bottle, holding it at the back of my mouth and praying it would quiet the flames in my throat. As I closed the medicine cabinet door, my reflection was bright red and the already round Irish face was twice as full. That was not just two chins I was seeing - it was many more.

Without any other option, I managed to get my husband's attention. We didn't say much to anyone but left our home full of extended family and drove to the local Emergency Room.

The care was solid, compassionate and patient. No one rushed me. I laid back, closed my eyes, allowed the hypnotizing strokes of a gentle understanding nurse, and imagined I was living in the moment two weeks earlier – me and my baby alive.

"Much of your pain is the bitter potion by which

the physician within you heals your sick self."

~ Khalil Gibran

November, 2001

The calendar marked a month since his death. For me it could have been that morning.

Time was an enemy. Each day, each minute, each heartbeat took me farther from him. My heartbeat was a source of constant agony. My empty arms were useless appendices reminding me of how much I had failed. They hung down at my sides as if they reach the ground. I curled them to my chest trying to turn back the clock to how he felt against my chest. It didn't work. The two times I held him he was full. I could feel his weight. Now, my arms kept wrapping until they were just around me. Pain wins. I have no choice but to allow it. I scratched my arms until they bled. I banged my head against the shower walls and I punched my stomach. I held my breath until blood vessels in my face burst.

Labor was so much easier. A drug was available to curb the raw pain. A nurse could apply pressure to your back. There was knowledge that the pain would end. It was not infinite.

There was nothing to take. Nothing to do. There wasn't even a word.

Pain, agony, excruciating. Each word just barely scraped the surface. What would the next month bring? Let alone the next heartbeat.

"Your tummy is getting bigger again, Mommy." My daughter wished aloud. Pushing against my belly she continued, "I think it is going to be a girl this time. " Not moving her hand off she looks at me and then back to my still protruding stomach. She pushed again. Then jumped "See it moved! I felt it kick!"

"No. There was no kick, Grace. There is no baby in there right now. I miss him too." With repressed tears and a lump in her throat that I can feel weighing down the pillow, my four year old rolled over. The hate she had for me in these moments were palpable. To get even, she would not let me rub her back. She didn't let me leave the room either. A four year old ashamed, embarrassed, and wanting to attack one of the very few people she was forced to trust.

Many times I did feel a kick. "Phantom pains." Phantom being the baby, I suppose. I was scared for when I wouldn't feel them anymore.

Very little at this time could hold my attention. In early November, an article caught my eye in one particular magazine and I picked it up. It was about a baby boy, a coarct, a surgeon, and brain damage. Much of the article I did not comprehend. I remembered the mother and wondered about her. Selfishly, I wondered if she would be willing to help me. Someone out there had some idea of what I had experienced. Though my son was gone, hers was still here. Maybe in connecting with someone who came close to this experience, I could find sense. Someone could tell me: "What do I do now?" I was so lonely.

I started by dialing the magazine, locating the author and getting whatever information I could. The only thing he could share was the lawyer's phone number. So, in my new reality that offered no template to live by, I went ahead and dialed the lawyer. Two rings and a deep voice spoke: "Jim Beasley." I had never heard of him before reading the piece. I appreciated the connection I felt with his first name. His last name meant nothing. Little did I know at the time I had direct-dialed a legendary plaintiff's attorney.

"Hello. You don't know me. *Philly Mag* gave me your phone number. My son died in October after surgery done by Norwood and I was wondering..."

My words were choppy through the tears unsuccessfully restrained. The lawyer took away some of my work by simply offering "I am so sorry." I lost my breath and fell deeper into the tears, as this was the first apology that was more than an expression of sympathy. Though I didn't realize at the time just how much this gentleman understood.

"That is the worst thing to happen to a parent. What is your son's name?"

So few times had I said his name. The conversation left the other boy and became all about my baby. It was wonderful to be able to speak freely. Even to a stranger. His wasn't the first query that included "What happened?" so, at this point I was getting better in reply, "I don't know and they don't either. But I have requested his records. I just want everything that was ever his. Maybe within the records there is an answer."

"I would like to help you if you would like."

He already had. He let me talk about my newborn son. The respect he showed my tears and James's memory was a welcome, if unexpected invitation, to stay. In addition to contact information, he instructed me to file an executor-ship at the local courthouse.

"I just want to know what happened," closed the conversation.

I organized my extra time with purpose. The day he died was for notification. Day two was arrangements. Day three was squaring finances to pay for the funeral. Day four was preparing for the burial. Day five was the funeral. Day six I signed two cards – an anniversary card to my husband and an official request for medical records. Everything that had James's name on it was mine by right if not by will. Medical records were one of the few possessions accumulated in eleven days. On a handwritten note went a directive:

"To Whom It May Concern:

Please send all medical records regarding our son James M. Mannix (date of birth - 10/2/01) to our home address listed below as soon as possible. James was a patient in the Nemours Cardiac Center. Please call if there are any questions or problems in getting this information to us within the normal 3 - 5 days. Thank you."

I signed with name, address, and phone number.

I waited anxiously. A thin manila envelope arrived standard mail a few weeks later. Yet, it was a very thin envelope. Inside, without a cover letter, were several pages of lab values. None of which made any sense to a preschool teacher without medical training. So I asked my sister. She'd been a nurse on an adult cardiac unit for twenty years. We had never before had any reason to discuss specifics of her work. Even after the preliminary in utero diagnosis, she didn't share any possibilities. Along with the choir of public opinion she offered, "Don't worry. Everything will be fine. If there was something to worry about they would tell you to worry." A coarctation of the aorta had a standard of care. It was not the life threatening heart defect of other syndromes where experimentations or compassionate care must be discussed.

Sure enough, I was not hearing concern from anyone. My OB just maintained the chant of "Oh he (Dr. Bhat, fetal echocradiographer) is the best."

The pediatrician offered agreement, "That is supposed to be the best place if you need help."

But this day, a month after this baby's death, upon first glance my RN sister's finger went directly to blood gas values listed under October 4, 2001 between 4PM and 7PM. "Why didn't someone do something? Why wasn't he reintubated?" she queried.

"What's reintubated?" I asked slowly as I stumbled over pronunciation. I called the lawyer from her kitchen phone. From our first conversation, Jim Beasley Sr. had given me his home phone number with the instructions to use it anytime.

He wasn't sure what to say himself, "Can you send me a copy of that? I can have someone review them for clarity. Perhaps, it is time to request records from our office."

I hesitated and astutely he caught me. "Mrs. Mannix you don't have to proceed."

"Well," I explained, "I have an appointment with the surgeon and cardiologist next week. Maybe they can clarify what happened. Maybe we really don't have to go any farther."

"Good plan. Keep that appointment. Let me know how it goes. If you wouldn't mind, I would still like to take a look at those records you received." No harm in that; one more person that may be able to offer an answer.

The doctors didn't say much of anything. At least nothing that hadn't been said the last time I was there – when James died. During our scheduled appointment with Drs. Bhat and Norwood, they revealed they would do everything exactly the same way if James presented to them again. They would do nothing different. They were as surprised by the downturn of events as I was. My husband asked about the Mortality and Morbidity meeting. They knew of no such meeting happening regarding our son's care.

So, trust came back into question. If I was to take them at their word, then no quality meeting was held to discuss the causes and outcomes of care provided at their hospital after the unexpected death of an otherwise healthy 8lb. 4oz. baby boy. If I were to trust the information they had shared as complete and truthful, then my son's death was the result of much unknown about his condition despite their strong confidence in making decisions without asking us while he was still alive.

If I chose to not believe their few words, there were more questions than answers. Every question would in fact lead to another one and another and another. The only thing I could walk away with is that trust should never be given as freely as when I had turned it over to the white-coated professionals just weeks earlier.

The physicians' blank stares were incomprehensible a month after my son's death. I only wanted James to be remembered. I tried to suppress the need for understanding and moved on to the need for memorial. I asked the social worker, "What can I do to help?"

The first response was really nothing more than a continuation of the shoulder-shrugged dismissal. And the latter came with a blank stare. "We'll call you."

She never called. Norwood's reputation for finding answers for the most complex of heart defects ran directly convergent to the quickly accepted answer that there was no answer to my baby's tragedy.

It was a frustratingly fruitless experience. Shortly after arriving home I called the lawyer. "Let's move forward."

Mr. Beasley would officially request the medical records from the hospital. Once they were recieved and his office did an official review he would be in touch. I was encouraged to call with any concerns or questions in the interim.

Patiently I waited. Well, every minute was an eternity, so to me I felt patient. Those around me at that time may have experienced it differently. The days passed with tears and anger, wonder and aching. I banged the phone receiver against the wall when I heard, "That's why they call it medical *practice*," or "He had a birth defect remember Mary Ellen," or the unforgivable offense to a mom who has buried her child: "Aren't you over that yet?" The worst ones were actually the ones that didn't mention him by name or allusion. The ones who wanted me to be able to act and speak as if nothing had happened. I could either be quiet and allow the elephant to be swept under the rug or I could speak up. I was left divided between the world of blissful ignorance and a world where babies die. I knew how to parent living children. Learning how to be the parent of a dead one was an unexpected and unwelcome challenge.

The sun shone everyday the Fall of 2001 despite the endless gray surrounding me. The presence of the countless innocent lives lost tragically that September worked to brighten the world for their greiving loved ones. Their spirits made the sunshine and clouds disperse. My baby boy kept the sky a brilliant blue. Together they all seemed to envelope the eastern seaboard in warmth uncharacteristic for the Fall. It was late November before any significant rain developed. Getting out of bed didn't seem an option most days. However, it was still a requirement of the mother of three surviving children. All I wanted to do was to return to the dead one. The one who was all alone somewhere. Days were filled with a robot making lunches, getting gas, and driving children to and from school. Fingernails were worn down from shovel-less grave digging.

Hair was used to strategically hide where I had scratched neck, head, and face in the shower.

The strangest words I heard repeatedly were, "You look so beautiful." A postnatal glow defied my reality. As fresh as childbirth made my skin, as healthy as the hormones made my hair and nails, a baby's absence made my existence ugly and unnecessary. The empty attic was a wonderful respite to attempt to hold my breath until there was no more feeling. I failed at all these activities. Clearly, I was good for nothing.

By mid December, the suburban landscape was filling with lights and holiday décor. My heart was nearly dead. I had muddled through Halloween collecting pitiful stares as my daughter collected candy. She called out "Trick or Treat" and the oblivious asked me, "So, where is the baby?" At Thanksgiving I managed to attend family dinners where no one mentioned the newest family member by name. I started each holiday graveside and it became increasingly difficult to see the world's return to normalcy. Trust and any remaining hope was evaporating quickly. I would have to choose a world.

There were a couple physicians who tried to keep me whole.

I was lying on the dining room floor next to my son's empty bassinet, kids were in school and the youngest living child was taking a nap. There were boxes of Christmas decorations to empty. Anything beyond thinking about it was futile. The phone rang. It was an annoying interruption to my active grief but strangely, also a welcome relief. Someone had at least dialed my number. As became my routine, the phone was ringing and slowly I gathered composure. Wiped away the tears and blew my nose.

I reached the phone and technology had identified the caller. It was the law firm.

The introduction was direct yet kind as the caller explained he was Mr. Beasley's son, Jim Beasley, Jr. "I am so sorry about your son. How are you doing?"

I could have replied truthfully:

"I am in such terrible pain. My son James was diagnosed in utero with coarctation of the aorta. He was given such amazing percentages for survival. They said 100%. Those were the "chances" they gave him for coming home – 100%. It was the only heart defect

he had. They said it is thee most treatable congenital heart defect. The doctors keep saying they don't know why James went into cardiac arrest while he was recovering from surgery. He was on a heart and lung machine for 4 days following surgery - crazy tubes coming straight out of his chest. He did get off that horrid contraption only to end up back on it 4 days later due to an emergency operation on his lung. The ventilator supposedly made his lungs "brittle." I would have told them to not operate if they had just given me the chance. I never left the hospital but once and they seemed to not even see I was there. He was born beautiful. I did get to hold him briefly but now my arms feel so useless they might as well be amputated. Can that be arranged? I keep trying to crawl into the bassinet. I am still too big. When I managed to go out, people still asked, "When is the baby due?" He never got to come home. I pumped my breasts the whole eleven days he was here. I still have some in the freezer. What do I do with it? Pour it down the shower drain with the other breast milk that comes out when I bathe? I can't stop crying at night. The sleeping pills aren't even working. I am blessed with three other children but it feels like a curse. If they weren't here, neither would I be. The only thing I can stand to listen to is a an old seventies tune. I miss my baby. I want him back! Can't I just dig him back out of his grave? I feel like my umbilical chord is still attached – but now grows out of me and leads to a grave."

Instead of scaring him away I managed, "Fine, thanks for asking."

He explained the reason for the call: "We have received your records and I have done an initial review. There is cause to move forward."

Immediately I had to figure out if I could trust him or if I could handle not trusting him. Since the initial phone call with his dad I had done some of my own research. I had the time. His dad was a legend. The son was a well-regarded attorney in his own right despite his youth. He could have been my brother. They were the same age and shared the same drive for achievement. Norwood was held in high regard by his peers too. That didn't do my son any good. Would the legal system serve James any better? For my sanity, I had to proceed. There was something about this dad and son that felt right. I still didn't trust myself so I would bring caution with every step. There wasn't anything this firm would do without me knowing it. I would also make certain they knew how beautiful and how missed James was.

Jim explained he would reach out to a couple physicians for expert opinions. It may take a little time but he would be in touch. In the interim, he would be available if I needed anything. The conversation ended with a strange, unexpected wave of calm. I didn't even bang the receiver when I hung up. Thank God I had somewhere to go. A doctor may have taken my son's life, but perhaps, a lawyer would save mine. I would realize later this lawyer was also a doctor.

Still, as he was reaching out, so was I.

There were a few students I had taught whose parents were physicians. One still lived and practiced in the Philadelphia area. Dr. Nick, as he is known, is a highly regarded orthopaedic surgeon. His skill in repairing the aches and pains of athletes and professional dancers is known around the country. His ability to practice in the high-risk orthopaedic specialty for decades without one filed complaint was meaningful to me. I called him.

I tried not to say too much. The calls were at night and in the day. It wasn't just one call. It was many. He listened. More than anything, he listened. I needed to make sure I wasn't allowing myself to become part of the problem by employing the tort system. Perhaps, it all "just happened." Perhaps there wasn't anything to get on public record. As we spoke, Nick was open and honest. I allowed trust. Nick had no stake in this claim in anyway. Yet, he still didn't know anything about pediatric heart surgery.

I dug a bit farther and reached out to a former parent who was a pediatric cardio-thoracic surgeon. He was not paid for his complete review of my son's records. He offered an unbiased and educated opinion. "Had your son been anywhere else in the world he would be alive today." There was something to learn. Perhaps gross medical negligence was a part of my son's life. Perhaps, the pediatric heart community had some skeletons that needed airing. Perhaps the hospital didn't realize all that was happening within it. It could be something else completely. I had the time and interest to investigate. Whatever it was, it became a defining stroke in my son's life. I had to know what "it" was.

The firm's building was impressive. It was a warm January night, well past regular business hours when I paid my first of many visits to "The Beasley Building". There were larger firms housed in much bigger buildings. It was the uniqueness of and appreciation for this building that gave me some comfort as to the approach a lawyer inside might take in fighting for my baby. The building was an old church. I was approaching from its rear. The backside of the building was a magnificent mural. There were builders and plans. A gray-haired man stood in the center holding architectural plans with a young woman at his side. To his lower right a younger man was crouched with a toddler with long dark hair in his arms. He was pointing up and her gaze followed his direction. Following her gaze I was looking at a painting of scaffolding and men working on a building. Walking around to the front, my gaze remained upward to follow the beauty of the building from mural to delicate façade. The windows were an elegant stained glass. Turning to the front of the building, the street lights revealed a gothic-style, church-like structure. My anxiety began to give way to a familiar ease. I knew this street.

Whatever this building was it was like many others I had sought refuge in over the years as an Irish Catholic. The entrance a deep-set, pointed arch recessed from the hustle of the center city street. The solid wooden doors were reminiscent of medieval England and things I'd admired at The Philadelphia Art Museum. If nothing else, this appointment was worth the aesthetic escape I was enjoying from my grief-stricken exile of the past few months. The door slowly opened to reveal a vestibule of gracefully carved woodwork, a regal full staircase, and the inviting warmth of mahogany. This was no fluorescent-lit, modern, flashy attorney's office. This was a hand picked space cared for by someone who spent a great deal of time there. If this wasn't a house, it was someone's second home. I began to feel like an invited guest not just a potential client. It would take me years of appointments to see and appreciate all the delicate, stately intricacies of the building. Fulfilling its original intent as a church, this building would become my refuge.

Accompanying me were my husband, a yellow container, and a promise to my son. In the container were a small blue photo album, the 2001 calendar, the simple diagram drawn by the cardiologist when a discrete coarctation was diagnosed, my notes on sticky pads from the operation, papers and literature from the hospital. The pain of my son's loss was still deep, raw and visible. I felt removed from the magnitude of my actions: keeping an appointment with Pennsylvania's premier medical malpractice attorneys with the intent to sue physicians, hospitals, and a health care system. I climbed a grand carpeted mahogany staircase. Though just a few flights, It was a healthy climb for the unfit. Led through just one corridor and one large tall walnut door, we arrived in a spacious office more like the sitting room of an old Main Line estate. As if in the Beasley kitchen, we sat around a large, circular mahogany table. I tried to catch my breath and keep my eyes focused. There was more stained glass than solid wall. Pictures of family and friends were easy to spot. An elderly gentleman welcomed us warmly and introduced himself, though now, I knew who he was. I had seen his picture and his desk in that magazine article a few months before.

He offered sympathy with an outstretched arm and gentle, weather beaten eyes, "Losing a baby is the worst thing in the world. Especially for a new mom." I had heard this many times before and had been disappointed by its standardization. Within a couple moments the speaker would usually add a comment that proved there was no real understanding of the magnitude of the loss. They all started with "but." "But when my mom died it was like the worse thing in the world. I can totally understand what you are going through."

"But at least you didn't have to bring him home."

"But everything happens for a reason."

With forced composure I acknowledged his kindness and waited for the letdown. He reached for my arm and went on, "It's like losing a limb. For a mom to lose a baby it's like losing a large piece of you. A part you can feel. It is a physical loss."

I tried not to cry but I wasn't in shock anymore. The tears could not be kept at bay. The old guy got it. He verbalized what I had been experiencing. It must have been the years in the business that gave him an edge. He would know just what to say. I chose to believe he knew what to say because he understood me. I had to start trusting someone again. In four years, I would learn I was right about the stately lawyer; and sad that I was.

He introduced his son. I remembered the voice from our phone call. He was an MD himself and would be working the case with his dad. Mr. Beasley explained, "Every case in our office gets two attorneys. This allows for availability in case of scheduling conflicts or the like." Sadly, that would prove necessary for our case as well.

*"Once in a while you get shown the light in
the strangest of places if you look at right."*

~ Robert Hunter

Early Spring was approaching as I sat, staring at the empty crib in the corner of the bedroom. The phone rang. I wiped away the tears, took a deep breath and answered with masked composure. Jim was calling to share the discussion he had with a physician familiar with pediatric cardiology and critical care who had reviewed James's records. What he was about to share would leave a scar as deep as anything Kochilas said on October 4th. Jim allowed for as much time as needed. He spoke, I questioned, he spoke, I was silent, he waited, I repeated his words, he listened, he spoke, I cried, he apologized and he empathized.

The expert found several concerns in James's care. Hearing her review was when I began to understand and accept that I did search for what my son needed. He did need an operation in infancy to treat the condition of his aorta. It was the actions of Norwood coupled with a broken system that sacrificed my son's life.

The expert physician agreed on the need for surgery. However, the approach and postoperative care James received was criticized. James had only an isolated coarctation within a normal arch, he would have done well with a less risky surgical approach. A left thoractomy (an incision into the left side of the chest cavity) could have addressed the repair without stopping his heart as the deep hypothermic circulatory arrest (cooling of the body's temperature to 32 degrees Fahrenheit) with cardiopulmonary bypass did. It would have been full informed consent if his parents had been told of this option. However, once the aggressive approach was taken he should have remained sedated and intubated (on a ventilator) overnight. He needed a chance to rest from the trauma of surgery. Unfortunately he was extubated (taken off the ventilator) electively within hours.

There were sparse records regarding the arrest. There were hours of blood gases and respiratory therapy records for the three hours between extubation and arrest. They showed without question carbon dioxide retention, hypoxia, and acidosis. These indicators demanded immediate re-intubation. Nothing was done and he suffered. Before James was extubated his arterial blood gases demonstrated carbon dioxide saturation (PCO2) of 52. The normal range is 40-45. His oxygen saturation (PO2) was 201 with a normal pH. Within minutes of extubation, the pH had dropped ten decimal points and the PCO2 rocketed to 69.3. The PO2 plummeted from 201 down to 63. All of these red flags occurred within a ten-minute window. PO2 is the oxygen flowing in your blood. PCO2 is the carbon dioxide. PH represents the acid balance in our blood. These are key indicators when blood gases are drawn to understand how the respiration and blood flow are cooperating.

I hung up the phone slowly. I had been anticipating, actually hoping, for the words, "Sorry we don't have a case.

They really did all they could. There is no explanation for what happened to your son." That would have been a great relief. Instead, I had learned that my instincts were true. My life's landscape continued to change. The law firm became a best friend.

I should have been put on medication or hospitalized. Five months after my son's death, family and friends had moved forward and were expecting me to be "over it," "better," or just "not so sad all the time." My sister called in the days after this talk with Jim Jr. I banged the phone against the wall repeatedly while she was still speaking. There is no way she could have understood the confusion and pain I was suffering. I had no way to explain it or handle mundane misunderstandings.

My world was only what I could see. I did not have to be or do anything for anyone else. I was losing the sanity and sense of balance in the world I had previously enjoyed. The world had irrevocably changed. I made sandwiches and got the kids to school on time. I showered and dressed. There was food on the table for dinner. I did the laundry. Each one of these benign activities was excruciatingly painful. During anyone of them it was work to not collapse. Every moment, I could feel the absence of one. With each step and breath, I was moving farther away from the time I spent with my baby. It was neglectful to continue living. There were no bottles or baby cereal. When the kids were dropped off at school there was no infant car seat or babysitter. There was no tiny laundry to fold. No cries to interrupt my shower. In sleep, my breasts would still leak.

I was losing faith in others. My faith in God was so roughly shaken I could no longer pray. Even the old memorized standbys from Catholic school just stuck. It was like having a broken car starter as my faith's driver. "Hail Mary," I would start and then say it again and again and a couple more times. Each time it would become shorter and shorter until I stopped even trying. I had prayed ceaselessly when there was a chance it could save James from death or even merely lessen his trauma. My prayers seemed more like the invocation of a curse. I dared not go on and risk more. Friends and family were well meaning and used their faith to excuse my son's untimely demise:

"God has a plan."

"God needed an angel."

"He is with God now."

This was not the God I knew. So, maybe I didn't know Him at all. I was now wrong about everything I had ever believed. I was unable to share why I felt so incredibly distraught and destroyed. The legal advice was to not mention specifics of the case, which meant not talking about James. His whole short life was now a potential lawsuit. When letters came home from my children's schools sent out to the three different school-wide communities, a knife would stick in my throat. All three read to the effect: "His/her baby brother died because of a weak heart at birth." James's heart was solid and strong. Without such a strong heart he wouldn't have survived the poor healthcare as long as he did. He was born with a great vessel that needed help. He died because he was a patient in a healthcare system failing little babies and many of their doctors. Not from any medical condition. To understand this but not be able to explain it added to the isolation from friends and family while adding to a reliance on the law firm. It would have been a great challenge to find the right words to describe the loss. Most people didn't give much credence to medical malpractice anyway. It was certainly not a popular approach to the death of a child in a hospital. If it was a criminal case, I would have been the defendant.

The experience was like being in "the hole" in a prison where I was to serve a life sentence. The crime was burying my own baby. I had thus been put in this hell. Openly grieving and discussing my infant son that died was reason to my being put in solitary. When James's name was mentioned, others' jerked their head away so quickly. The disengaged and annoyed looks were invisible whips that left an everlasting sting.

I knew I was not alone. My new best friends were with me. Each in her own private hell. We would never have known of each other if we hadn't been the vehicles through which a crime against nature was committed. I could not see my companions's faces except the lady in the cell next to mine. We got a glimpse of each other's tears through the crack at the bottom of the steel, reinforced, locked door. She was a key to survival. Her baby's name was Dylan. I felt another sting.

I heard all of their heart-wrenching cries. Occasionally one of us would rise out of agony long enough to give some small, gentle, priceless, measure of comfort to another. Curled in balls of battered flesh on cold wet cement floors that were disguised with mattresses and bedspreads we cried and screamed out our babies' names. The walls are paper-thin but there was no strength to break through. The walls that barricade us from the outside are solid, soundproof, impenetrable. None of the cries, sobs, pain were reflected on the other side. People out there were kept safe from this hideous reality: a tiny, little perfect, beautiful baby rests in a casket, not a crib.

I agreed to file the official complaint. I was now a pawn in someone else's chess game. My life became the war's collateral damage. Bounced back and forth between courts and political climates, I was a ricocheting bullet that left damage to all on any near landscape. What I needed discussed legally was the last act that the surgeoun performed on my child without permission. It was done with the intent to harm. It may be something I can never prove. Yet, I have learned to trust my maternal instincts. They have always been right.

If you file a complaint in Pennsylvania of medical negligence, malpractice or wrongful death in civil court, the complaint must be accompanied by expert, documented opinions after review of the records. This is the responsibility of the plaintiff. Reasonable cause must be demonstrated. Before the complaint enters into a court, the plaintiff's counsel is expending a significant amount of cash. It was the hospital's charge for the copying and delivery of records. The more complex the care, and the longer the stay the more expensive the case will be. The expert, who as a physician, is already limited on time, is paid an hourly rate. At the outset, a lawyer has to not only be convinced of the negligence, but also confident of its validity to a potential jury. Five grand to start. It quickly goes up from there.

It was scary, almost an embarrassment, to mention I was suing a doctor and hospital. It remained a very private affair. For the times that it was difficult to not mention the case, I would try to explain why. Eyes would look away. The topic of conversation would quickly be changed. It was particularly trying for my obstetrician.

Despite having previously mailed letters to my state representative on his behalf, now that I had engaged a lawyer in my son's care, the doctor became terse and seemed hesitant to see me as a patient. Just a week before learning of the pregnancy, I was diagnosed with cervical carcinoma in situ. Precancerous lesions. Once the baby was discovered, there was nothing to do for the previous diagnosis. The baby's healthy delivery would have to come first. As my immune system shut down to help the pregnancy survive, the alien bodies were free to strike more aggressively. By the time I was able to address the issue, it had taken over a large portion. Surgery was needed. The day after Christmas 2001, my long time obstetrician performed outpatient surgery. All things considered, it went well. I, of course, wished I never woke up.

A month post surgery, I was doubled-over in pain feeling like I was in labor. Clearly I had lost my mind. As my monthly period witnessed the absence of any newborn life around me, my mind must be so confused it produced a psychosomatic reaction. The blood came in gushes. In one gush three pads were soaked. My pants were red to my knees.

Hours would pass, sometimes days, before the next gush. The pain was constant yet always most intense right before the gush. I was able to time the waves of pain and intensity to the same rhythm that my labor pains were timed in real childbirth. Each gush gave some relief for a short period. For the first few months, it lasted 2-4 days. By month 7 and 8, it was a bi-monthly occurrence and could last as long as a week. I barely made it through my workdays. When at home, Percocet and Vicoden took the edge off enough that I would be knocked out for a few hours. I couldn't use these relief aids when having to work or drive children anywhere - which was most days. It caused great disappointment for many people. I reached out to my doctor throughout this time period for guidance and relief. After two years of calls and appointments, my doctor marched into the exam room thirty minutes late and firmly declared, "Look. You need to just get pregnant and get a stitch or have the hysterectomy already." After 14 years, there was no greeting. No warmth. He was done.

During my very first exam for a second opinion, the specialist examined me and almost yelled, "Jesus, you're all scarred. You have cervical stenosis." Years of pain, months of lost work, endless disappointments faced by my children, a lot of money spent on painkillers, several additional corrective procedures, a premature delivery, subsequent seven day NICU stay, and eventually a total abdominal hysterectomy all were the result of a previous cervical surgery. It didn't mean anything went wrong during the surgery. He did what he needed to do. Understood. War was never claimed or even considered. Sadness prevailed. Another trust misused. Even more so, faith and hope were disappearing like elaborate sandcastles at high tide.

Jim passed the official complaint in James's wrongful death case to me for review before filing. I had only minor thoughts as this was beyond my education and experience. He was gracious in answering questions and patient in explaining steps taken. Whereas there were months to prepare my family and I for medical treatment, the hospital and providers did not take advantage of the time to inform me. To give me a chance to ask the questions I needed to ask. Now, during the lawsuit, I was receiving an education that would benefit law provider as well as law student. It would be an education that would go one for years.

It was overwhelming to see the names of all the defendants on the complaint: The Jefferson Health System, The Nemours Foundation, A.I. DuPont Hospital for Children, Dr. William I. Norwood, Dr. Russell Raphaely and several other physicians. The main office for the first listed defendant was in Philadelphia. It made perfect sense. Born in one county, parents residing in another county, transferred to a neighboring state, the complaint should be filed within the limits of the health system I entrusted my son to. It was their relationship with these providers that steered James's care. Fate certainly couldn't ask me to go back to that neighboring state for a trial. Murphy's Law could. Act 13 was passed in Pennsylvania the same week our complaint was filed. The recently enacted statute required all medical malpractice lawsuits to be filed within the county where the injury occurred. James's case would be argued in Delaware. While the war was still on, it was a battle lost. I really couldn't do anything right.

After Jim's call informing me of the change in venue, I paid a visit to the cemetery. The ground was wet which gave way to my fingers. I tried to get him out of the ground and finally carry him home. It was only tears that escaped under a tree in the Angels section of Sts. Peter and Paul Cemetery. Sensibility beat out my passion as my fingers began to hurt and my clothes had become uncomfortably wet. When I stopped to breath, there was a very small hole dug only an inch or two wide with a similar depth. A shovel-bearing gravedigger who had taken shelter under a tree was staring at me. I gave up with the macabre. The promise, however, was renewed. I would find out what happened and learn what could be done better for the next young patient. Regardless of where I had to go or how long it would take.

In the 20th century play, "Socrates Inquires," the ancient philosopher debates the best candidate to oversee "the health of the people" with Aristodemus, a Spartan warrior. After having missed a landmark battle becuase of illness he was disenfranchised but still devoted to his country. For a time he was referred to as "Aristodemus the coward." An oracle convinced him to sacrifice his daughter's life would ensure the preservation of his society. Despite his success and becoming a king, he committed suicide over his daughter's grave some years later. After establishing that one man should be responsible for the physical well-being of the State the two deliberate just what kind of person that should be:

Socrates: "I suppose that this man, then, should be someone who himself knows about health and sickness?"

Aristodemus: "The man who knows something about health and sickness will have ideas about these subjects, and so he will not come to his task with an open mind."

Socrates: "He should not be a doctor then?"

Aristodemus: "Certainly not."

Socrates: "You would not see the same objection to a lawyer?"

Aristodemus: "No, on the contrary, a lawyer would be very suitable."

It took nearly a year after the funeral before there was anything prescriptive to do as the mother of a dead child. My head was held low and my conversation was tinged in anger. Support groups felt inadequate. Michael and I rarely looked at each other anymore. It was a welcome reprieve the first summer when I was asked to answer the defendants' interrogatories. Once the complaint was drafted, filed, and accepted in the court system, the defendants had a right to answers from their own set of questions. It was the plaintiff's duty to speak first in a multi-step process to secure information. The Beasleys never led me to believe it would be anything but a long, cold, arduous journey. I had visions of golf clubs as weapons with me as their instigator in violent pursuit of the surgeon. I was reluctant to admit to these daytime nightmares. The interrogatories gave me a job and focus. I grabbed a pencil as my shovel to dig through the legal papers. The sun swaddled me in warmth as I reviewed the eight-page list of questions.

I would have no control over the speed at which the court moved, but for such small tasks as this, delay was not an option. Despite a year of being unable to focus long enough to read a magazine article let alone a book, I could comprehend the legalese. Hospital and funeral home bills were collected and attached. My surviving children's names, our address, and places of James's birth, hospitalization and death were written repeatedly on the same document. Despite obvious answers, every mundane query was obliged despite the idiocy. Pages and pages of questions regarding James were simply unanswerable. My lack of knowledge on the subject was excruciating.

"What did he do for a living?"

"How many children did he have?"

"Was the decedent married at the time of his death?"

"State the respective names, ages, addresses, present whereabouts and relationship and marital status of the parties alleged to be dependent next-of-kin at the time of his death."

"State the gainful occupation which all of these dependent next-of-kin are engaged."

"Did the decedent leave surviving him any children?"

"From whom, on what date and in what amounts did the decedent receive any pay, wages, earnings or other compensation during the five years prior to his death?"

"Did decedent ever serve in the Armed Forces?"

"What was the decedent's physical condition prior to five years preceding his death?"

I wanted to know those answers. I was wishing that my son would have lived long enough to create them. After an hour of reading and re-reading in the hopes I must have missed something, I wondered how I would ever deal with not having the answers. The pain was raw. A grief counselor had explained the irony of my grief situation. No one knows how to deal with the death of a baby. If I had a need I would have to find the strength to ask for it. I would have to find my own support. The people on my speed dial were just as unprepared as I. With good intentions and whole hearts, they tried to resolve it for me quickly. This led to increased frustration and despondence. Everyone's answers and ideas seemed like clichés from an old "after-school special." Expectations, boundaries and limitations were defined through those conversations. It was like being in a virtual straightjacket. The absences and lack of returned calls or visits in the previous year, made it clear no one really wanted to hear my grief. I called the only person who didn't minimize my concerns despite the presence of emotion.

I wanted to say a lot. Like, "I would love to answer these questions, Jim. You know James would probably have had two kids but not until later in life because of his professional studies. He would have been a college professor, or an art historian. No, no. Had he been given safe, quality care he would have become a doctor. He would have grown up to help some other child the way he was helped. He loved the color blue and macaroni and cheese but would not go a day without reading the same Curious George book morning, noon, and night." I knew nothing of the sort. I didn't manage to say much. I didn't have to.

Present and prepared, Jim anticipated the call. My anger receded as he spoke with an edge, "They have so many attorneys over there, they probably have some god-forsaken clerk sending this stuff out without even looking at the content of the complaint." He said, "Don't bother with it. We'll make sure they know this is about the death of your baby. This is just stupid all that stuff they have in there. It's a form letter." My resolve was strengthened. It appeared a defense team that was most likely well-schooled and well-paid were asking things they knew I could not answer. More time to be wasted just in showing them the lousy job they were doing.

For each unanswerable question, Jim succinctly replied ad nauseum," Please read the Complaint. Plaintiffs' decedent was a minor."

The porch I sat on when I read those papers was sold with the rest of our first home later that year. A farm house in the middle of an inner suburb; we were closer to the city than any farm. It was single with a detached garage. A picket fence framed the backyard. The porch swing was favorite respite. If James wouldn't grow up there, none of his siblings would either. Besides, with our house in threatened foreclosure after medical bills, loss of work, and deep grief, there was little choice. If we had to front the cash for James's case, I would have been silenced along with James. This book would have been impossible.

PART II

"Yes, hell exists. It is not a fairy tale. One indeed burns there. This hell is not at the end of life. At the beginning.

Hell is what the infant must experience before he gets to us."

~ Dr. Frederick LeBoyer

Discovery is hearing what a witness chooses to share. It is receiving the medical records that risk managers decide to release. It is hesitantly sharing the army of experts and standards aligned in your camp. Depositions were opportunities for all the parties involved to reunite per court directives. The only people who speak are usually the deposed and the opposing counsel. Jim invited the deposed to participate in a "conversation like we are all around a dinner table only there is a court reporter taking down everything stated."

The first deposition in James's case was on a brilliant warm Spring day. At a time when James should have been learning to walk, I was becoming more confident in my legal steps. We met Jim in the foyer at the far end of the hospital. He gave us simple instructions while putting the notepaper and pen I brought in his briefcase. "Please, you won't need that. I will be taking notes and share them all with you. Ok? You guys okay?" Trust was being demanded. I was either all in or not. Wearing a simple black dress and clinging onto James's socks, I followed Jim and led my husband into the boardroom. Michael was a shell. I was little more. It was unclear how we held up since we could no longer lean on the other. My armor would have to be the attorney who shared James's name and the strength of a well-established firm. Time would tell how well the armor I chose would protect my frailties. A long rectangular mahogany table, fine Persian rug, oil portraits, anxious anticipation and untapped emotions crowded the otherwise empty room. This was the first day of freshman year.

A defense lawyer extended an unwelcome, repugnant greeting. I looked to Jim, he nodded ever so slightly towards me as he extended his hand and pleasantries to people that were refusing to tell me what happened to my son. I managed a stiff "Hello." This would be an uneasy exercise of shiny, polished, and polite fronts while my insides were damaged and terrified. After the move, after the Make A Wish Memorial Birthday party fundraiser, and after a second set of holidays without him, with a court reporter in place, some questions may be answered with the help of someone who had never even met my sweet, baby James.

"Dr. Raphaely, good afternoon. I'm Jim Beasley."

"How do you do?" the doctor asked.

"I'm doing well. How are you?"

"Fine, thank you," Dr. Raphaely replied with the confidence of previous experience.

"We're here to talk about James Mannix." Jim continued with some ground rules about being deposed and acknowledging materials received, "What is your present title if you will?"

"I'm co-director of the Nemours Cardiac Center and an anesthesiologist/intensivist in that center."

"Who is the other director?"

"Dr. Norwood."

Further placed into evidence was Raphaely's curriculum vitae and experience. None of which was impressive since my memory of this man was his inability to answer my questions with anything but variations of "I don't know" accompanied by shoulder shrugs.

Jim pressed on closer to what I was wanting: "Are there different requirements from a postoperative ventilatory management standpoint between infants and children?"

Without hesitation he replied, "Not in my eyes."

"How about between infants and adults," Jim asked.

"I don't see that there are major differences."

"In the October 2001 time frame at Nemours, was there a weaning protocol in place for infants that have just undergone cardiac surgery?"

"No," Raphaely definitively replied.

Jim was obliged to push, "How then would the physician at A. I. DuPont Hospital/Nemours, in the October of 2001 time frame determine when it would be appropriate to extubate a post-cardiac surgical infant?"

"By obtaining a history, performing a physical examination, evaluating the laboratory data, analyzing the data, coming to a conclusion, and then exercising judgment," the doctor replied.

The conversation continued between two gentlemen with occasional polite interruption from the defense counsel or the stenographer striving for accurate spelling. A superficial respect perhaps was present, but would any accountability show up?

Ever patient and willing to listen, Jim had fielded my calls and emails regularly on medical terms and legal proceedings. I knew now that intubation was when the breathing tube was put down James's throat. In turn, extubation was when the breathing tube was removed from his throat. James's "history" included our pregnancy and his hospitalization. Acidosis was a part of James's history too. Acidosis had something to do with blood gases, metabolism, and his recovery from surgery. Most importantly, James's history included a full-term pregnancy, healthy delivery, and being 8 lbs. 4 oz. at birth. Whereas I was wearing my heart on my sleeve, my lawyer was reserved and professional. Seeing him selecting words chosen for my son and I, in particular, allowed my trust to flow a bit more freely.

Jim was able to converse with the doctor in a physician's language: "Was there a window, if you will, of approximately how long after a median sternotomy and deep hypothermic circulatory arrest in the October 2001 time frame that would typically pass before the patient was extubated?" A median sternotomy is the cut down the middle of the chest and through the breastbone. Deep hypothermic circulatory arrest is collection of big words to describe purposefully freezing the body to create a bloodless theater for open-heart surgery. Jim was searching for more information about the open-heart surgery James endured that I never understood they were even doing until well after they had already begun.

Raphaely's answer was cloaked in medical jargon, "The time period is usually anywhere from three to six hours. We look for certain features and in terms of – one, is does the data indicate that the circulation has responded favorably to the operation; secondly, is there any – what is the magnitude of mediastinal drainage from the wound; and thirdly, is the patient's body temperature in all areas at normal values." The mediastinal drainage was the fluid from the chest cavity collected post surgery in the bubbling old coffee-percolator-like contraption at the foot of the isolette.

My breath began to escape me. These words I had only ever heard after his death. The lawyer had helped me to understand. The "repair procedure" that James underwent had the surgeoun making an incision down the center of his chest, sawing and spreading the breastbone to give access to the cardiac region. James was cooled below 20 degrees Fahrenheit, his heart was stopped and a machine was hooked up to his major arteries to oxygenate the blood while he was "at rest." This was a deceptive phrase as his body was really being traumatized. The body is cooled below freezing so circulation stops in hopes the brain will be minimally affected when the heart stops beating during the surgery. The standard approach that could have helped James's condition was a left thoractomy

– an incision is made through the patient's left side and no deep hypothermic circulatory arrest is needed.

A tube was placed down James's newborn throat to allow for mechanical ventilation. His eyes were taped shut. Intubation, or re-intubation, was the process of having the tube properly placed (or re-placed) for mechanical ventilation to be successful. It would be a tough visual for any mom. Yet, most parents will agree to whatever is necessary to save your child's life. It was our right and the providers' responsibility for Michael and I to have been told all available, known options for the treatment of his condition. We were not told.

I drifted from October 2001 to the current day and time and back again several times. Jim was consistently looking across the table, hunched over a yellow tablet prepared to write. He paused thoughtfully, made eye contact with the deposed then continued, "I'm at a disadvantage because I don't practice critical-care medicine, so my questions may be somewhat inarticulate. But as far as looking at the blood gas, you say you look at the pH, oxygen, hematocrit, base excess, and various salts. When you are looking at the pH, what are you looking for?"

"Well, the normal range is 7.35 to 7.45, but with experience we've learned that there are ph's that – even though outside the normal range, biologic systems continue to function acceptably," the doctor said. Had I been allowed in the room, I would have been able to share when James's biologic systems were not functioning acceptably. The maternal bond was screaming. The defense would hide behind these highly-technical terms in their argument. It would successfully confuse all but those with at least three years of formal medical training. Ph, hematocrit, all these variables were critical factors in James's history. The neonate body works dependent on each of its systems. As complex as the professionals worked to make it sound, James simply was not getting enough oxygen. Jim had to maintain his composure to listen closely to where the defendants were leading us astray. Point by point though every deposition each defendant would be guided cheerfully by Jim down a road that narrowed with each question until, finally, there was no answer but the reason why James died: he was being denied necessary oxygen. But that would be a long time coming.

"Are those ranges which differ from the 7.35 to 7.45 kind of an experienced-based thing?" Jim asked. Raphaely answered in the affirmative and went on to point to textbooks and journals that addressed this issue. He included an adult textbook, Holbrook, which he applies some of its principles to children. Having an MD ask these questions was reassuring and fortunate. As much as this physician would try to confuse the issue, Jim was able to bring him to task. Ranges in blood values became the focus. According to Raphaely, a normal range for a "few day old infant's" carbon dioxide saturation levels would be a little lower than in adulthood. "Say somewhere between 32 and 37."

Jim proceeded past the event of October the fourth, the early extubation, the rising carbon dioxide levels and falling oxygen saturation. He moved on through alveolar function and actelactasis. A review of the daily happenings of the following week was in place. I would have to reread this information later with a medical dictionary to understand.

"Now let's see. On the 11th there's another note, 14:45. Would you mind reading that into the record?"

As the defendant began reading he tripped over his own penmanship acknowledging at a point, "I can't read my own writing."

Jim was asking his final impressions. In the early part of his deposition Raphaely acknowledged James's postoperative course should have ran 5, maybe 7 days. No more than 10. When asked if there would have been restrictions placed on James postoperatively the answer was "No."

"Was October 11th the last interaction you had with James?"

"I can't be sure what – do you know what- I need to consult a calendar to see when the 11th was, what day of the week?"

Shoulders still hunched over the legal pad with pen in hand Jim's head turned towards me. The rest of the audience followed his gaze. Finally, I could speak.

My gaze locked on Raphaely, "Thursday," I said. The attorneys seated on either side of the defendant began to open their mouths as if to object. Silence. This was a surprise maneuver. The inner machinations were evident as they scrambled for an appropriate objection. There was none. In one word the defense had been put on notice they were looking at a team across the table. And, I had a solid recollection of the events.

Raphaely cleared his throat and turned back to Jim "I probably then had some interaction on the morning of the 12th if I was still there and covering the ICU."

One of Jim's last questions for Raphaely, which would come up at all of the depositions was: "Did you ever develop an understanding as to the cause of James's passing?"

He skidded over this one, "I think – I don't recall specifically what I thought it was at the time. I don't recall." Raphaely continued to share that if there were any meetings discussing James's care he was not a party to them. "We have a conference now that occurs every Monday. It didn't occur as regular in the 2001 time frame as it does for the institution now." For me, there was the glimmer of hope that James's death was not in vain. Perhaps, just perhaps, the new Monday conference schedule was influenced a bit by my baby's suffering. Maybe he had made a difference.

We walked out into the late afternoon squinting our eyes. Though certainly worthwhile this deposition provided little more than being my initiation into civil litigation.

Depositions were all in part - a piece. We drove the silent ride north on 95, stopping at the cemetery on our way home. We stood there, separate, looking down in tandem at a small black granite block embedded in the ground with our son's name on it. There were no words. There would be no embrace. Our actions would never bring him back. They would however create an understanding of what happened and how to keep it from happening to someone else. That is the hope that kept me going. When we got home, I ate. Food was my only comfort, yet it kept me hollow.

Victims and families of preventable medical error do not usually remember everything about the event. People assumed I was so overwrought by emotion that there is no room to subscribe detail to memory. My hormones and the unbreakable bond between new mother and child kept me alert to every experience. It is the same structures that made the time after he passed so destructive.

The end of another school year came and went before we were in the same room speaking to the younger associate surgeoun involved in James's case. It was summer and my birthday was days away. The indulgence into James's world was my gift to myself. There was nothing worth celebrating. Yet, this doctor's testimony was benign. He was a puppet. Despite his intelligence, he would struggle to form a thought of his own. Without much ado, he was released from the case.

During an unseasonably warm spell, discovery of a whole other sort came in February 2004. The sun shone bright through my kitchen window and reflected television screen. The news report was concise. Federal marshals had recently escorted Norwood, John Maher MD, and a cardiac center administrator away from A.I. DuPont Hospital for Children. Many other sets of parents were grieving the loss of trust, health, and for some, even their children's lives.

Allegations were that without full informed consent the Nemours Cardiac Center and its physicians were utilizing experimental devices on the youngest of its patients. The device did not yet carry FDA approval. As I understand it,

Norwood lost his job and in time his license to operate expired. My long held suspicions held true - Norwood was facing many more lawsuits than just mine.

They would eventually number in the double digits in my region. Many of these cases would be filed in federal court. I hoped for the plaintiffs that such a strategic variance offered more protection for a victim's rights. I hoped somewhere Norwood would understand what all these families were struggling with.

"The reasonable man adapts himself to the world; the unreasonable one persists in trying to adapt the world to himself.

Therefore all progress depends on the unreasonable man."

~ George Bernard Shaw

Mid 19th-century European physician, Dr. Ignac Semmelweiss exposed the importance of hand washing, personal hygiene and, sterile hospital environments. After two rejections for a sought-after residency position, Dr. Semmelweiss applied for an obstetrics residency. Though not a highly regarded specialty, the location of the training was at a much-esteemed establishment in the mid 1800's - The Kraukenhaus in Vienna. Dr.Semmelweiss was a young doctor whose mother died in the weeks before his residency began. His father died shortly thereafter.

At the Kraukenhaus, the doctor was about to see much more death than he ever anticipated. Puerperal fever was a death sentence to hundreds of thousands of postpartum mothers. So closely associated with this population, it garnered the tag, "Childbed fever."

In the Kraukenhaus of 1840-1850, the First Division of the hospital was for lower-class mothers to deliver their children, and for residents to practice. Laboring moms would walk great distances, be assigned a bed and work to deliver their child. The residents would autopsy the dead from the previous day (pathology was a new, required course in Vienna) and immediately go to the First Division where they examined and delivered new infants. There were no sterile practices for doctors or their instruments.

Physicians were going from one laboring mother to the next performing internal exams with the same unwashed instruments and unprotected hands used to autopsy cadavers. Through careful observations and a willingness to think in a new way, Dr. Semmelweiss discovered the value of chlorine. After requiring all medical attendants to wash their hands in a bowl of chlorine liquid before touching a woman in labor, the deaths for puerperal fever dropped form 485 in the First Ward to only 56 in the first seven months of the following year. This was recognized throughout the medical community. Where there once seemed no hope when a mom was diagnosed with childbed fever, he had found a cure if not a prevention. He did so while facing great resistance from elder, more experienced physicians. His immediate supervisor rejected the notion that hand washing played a role in the deaths of his patients. It may have been just too threatening to consider that doctors were the cause of their own patients' deaths. Though he had great support amongst a few of his young peers, there was strong resistance from physicians with power and influence. Dr. Semmelweiss died shortly after being admitted to an insane asylum. The resistance remained. Today proper hygiene remains an integral factor in saving lives in hospitals despite a continued resistance. (Nuland)

Norwood created a three-step approach for children born with the most life-threatening of heart defects – Hypoplastic left heart syndrome (HLHS) to potentially save their lives. The Norwood procedure is a series of three separate surgeries over time to redesign the heart and great vessels to create adequate blood flow. HLHS is an underdeveloped left side of the heart. Surgeons would explain it as if the child was born with only half a heart because one side is so drastically underdeveloped. As recent as the 1980's, the only option for a terrified parent was compassionate care. Norwood brought another option. It seemed to me that where Dr. Semmelweiss was maintaining the health of all at the risk of no one; Norwood was maintaining his career at the risk of many. In particular, the economics driving an increase in the most expensive surgery – open heart bypass to increase income and for Norwood the more he could say he performed, the stronger his research studies numbers would be. To save the lives of the HLHS patient, many other CHD babies born with less threatening defects were made to face open heart when it did not have to be the only option. "Coarct babies' had a options. To have never been given any of them was like having my child kidnapped. Treatment for James's condition was established and standard. Instead, it seemed James was treated per the doctor's needs and not his own. Was this progress?

Years were passing. James's second Make-A-Wish birthday party fundraiser came and went. Though it was financially successful it did little to relieve my need to find out what happened to James. It did even less to reunite me with the family and friends I was drifting apart from, almost violently so. Each step that gave more clarity as to what really happened to James was like adding pieces to a puzzle. As hard and tiring as puzzle-work is, with each piece correctly assembled the anticipation builds to be able to see the complete picture. There is a myth that anger drives a lawsuit. The reality is that needs are its driver. Revelations are its fuel. Attorneys are the vehicles through which a resolve comes. I had to complete this puzzle.

My goal was attendance at every deposition. Fate would have different plans. Less than two months post partum from delivering my youngest child, I would be unable to fly four states away. James's brother is three years younger than him. James's grandfather had also died after a long, unexpected stay in a hospital after diagnosis of a similar congenital heart defect. Michael was worn. So, was I. And so was Jim. After a great deal of losses in each of our families, there were shared, bittersweet celebrations just prior to this visit to Rhode Island. Mike enjoyed the flight with Jim piloting up to this deposition. How he felt with defense's counsel in tow was unquestionably awkward. I was okay to have missed that flight. I didn't much care for defense counsel and in a couple months as the target of her questioning, I would really be disgusted. It is a unique dance opposing counsel performs. They have to work in tandem while cautiously not tipping a hand.

But, I did want to hear this particular physician's testimony in person. This is the physician who said he was sorry. This was the physician that came back to check on us. He never provided any answers or insights. I didn't necessarily recall a specific apology. Just a human and courageous expression of empathy for the tragic situation our newborn son was unexpectedly facing. This was not at all what the remainder of the care team was providing. We were left to chase them. It was an unfortunate way to obtain the information he had to share. At the time of filing the lawsuit, I personally requested that this doctor, Kochilas, not be named as a defendant. He had said he was sorry. He wasn't involved with the lack of information before and at consent. Nor was he a party to the final operation that was never consented to, yet guaranteed James's rapid decline. I believed that if I looked into his eyes as he answered Jim's questions, I would know a truth.

Kochilas had information about James during those hours that took the birthday parties, Gymboree, athletic events, sisters, and brothers out of James's life. He knew the play-by-play of James's medically induced trauma. Unfortunately, Kochilas was a victim to the lack of informed consent the surgeon provided. With surgery over, there were still hurdles. Since we were not aware of anything, everyone became suspect. The only way Kochilas would share testimony was to list him as a defendant. With years and deaths having passed between the memory of a warm-hearted physician and the revelations uncovered, I begrudgingly agreed.

There was someone else. Another doctor. Another gentleman, young, raising a family, and full of heart. His reaction to my call and requests was an immediate yes to help me understand what happened to my baby. He held no stake in my son's case. His was the objective and trained opinion that would serve as a strong base to move forward. Because of the actions of a highly recognized professional in the medical field, I had reason to question the authenticity of every highly regarded professional regardless of the specialty. I wanted to make certain the firm wasn't creating a case when perhaps there really wasn't one. Perhaps my son did just die without earthly explanation as the hospital team was presenting. I survived my nights by trying to understand what happened. The mothers of other heart babies helped me understand how odd the series of events that made up my son's life and death actually were. One heart mom whose baby lived his last six weeks in the hospital was especially taken back when looking at the small collection of photos I had of James.

"Is this James?" she asked as she pointed to a photo of my husband feeding James from a bottle.

"Oh, yes." I replied with a sigh.

She replied with hushed surprise and almost disbelief.

"No really that is James," I retorted. "the older kids' baby pictures are over here."

"Oh no. I know this is James. But he was eating?"

"Well, yeah. At least until the surgery. It wasn't until the events after the surgery that things went so far aground that he couldn't eat."

Unknowingly she guided me, "Mary Ellen. Heart babies. Who are sick. Are *not* eaters. They are too tired for that."

I began to share more of his pictures. Disbelief that he was a sick child reigned; especially among heart families. As I listened to increasing numbers of parents share the story of their deceased heart babies more and more holes in James's care and his physicans's explanation of his passing revealed themselves. His entire course of treatment was questionable. Despite the easily identified preventable errors that plagued James's early treatments, it would be his last day that would haunt me.

Many will rally around Norwood and question my intentions. The joy in their lives is immeasurable, thanks to some of his work. These are parents whose children are alive or lived longer than expected because of the Norwood procedure. There is no discount on the enormity of the discovery and development of this three-stage procedure to save lives that would otherwise have only one option. Norwood has a solid understanding of how the heart works, how it develops, and how it can even be "re-worked" to successfully perform its function. Through a combination of training, intelligence, creativity, and diligence Norwood served his profession well. Somewhere along the line something went wrong. Unable or unwilling to self-actualize and consider how "poor outcomes" may have resolved more successfully in his own work, patients and families like me have had to investigate it ourselves.

The review received from my personal outreach for help in understanding was troubled by all of James's care. Carefully he chose his words, "I would never, nor do I know another in my field, that would place a child in that critical state back on 'baby bypass' for a lobectomy. That is not necessary. With a child in such a critical condition." He stopped. I understood. Norwood had expert understanding of the inner workings of a neonatal chest.

The surviving children survived with parents half what they once were. We all managed to get by. I maintained trust and critical analysis by checking in monthly with the firm. Jim and his dad were overseeing the case. The civil law world moves like molasses, yet not as sweet. There were motions back and forth. Some motions won and some lost. Though it was discouraging, it was not the end. These actions were all taken in stride.

Each Fall was a revisit of the Fall 2001. I struggled through the golden days and beginning of school as the memories began to creep up and attempt to swallow me whole. I was powerless against the calendar each Fall. As kind as friends and family were they just didn't want to know how much I missed my son. Even less was the interest in understanding that the baby died as a result of dangerous behavior within the medical establishment. I wrote about the anguish while still raw from grief. Since the lawsuit was ongoing, I had only one person I knew I could safely share this with – Jim. He may not have read any of my musings yet he commented with compassion on every one. It was good to share it. It was good to have someone, somewhere that wasn't pleading with me to stop being so sad. I would have preferred joy as well. I just wasn't there yet.

"What we have once enjoyed and deeply loved we can never lose,

for all that we love deeply becomes a part of us."

-Helen Keller

I called Jim one early Fall afternoon to "check in". The lawyer was one of the places I felt his memory and my grief were "safe". The sky was its brilliant blue and a few treetops where gold. The paralegal answered with a sigh, "Oh Mary Ellen." Immediately, I knew something was wrong. Not intending to be invasive but out of concern I asked, "Is Jim okay?" It was a week before James's second birthday, September 25, 2003.

"Jim's at the hospital with his wife. The baby died," the paralegal cautiously shared.

Oh no. No. No. This was not the connection anyone wanted or needed. Dear god.

His wife. His kids. Picking out clothes and a casket. Telling people. Recognizing a birthday that wasn't. In one minute, two years went by and it seemed they would be uniquely repeated now in Jim's life. The grim reaper's baton had moved on. I had been commemorating this as James's time, but it was now Tommy's.

Tommy's time was much more than these late September days. When asked, his mom would take a deep breath, speak in a gentle tone of the years before he was born. The story of how they came to be. Every one begins long before their birthday. Liz started with meeting Jim in college. How they both shared an intrigue in medicine. How she trained to be an obstetrician. And, how for the love of her family she walked away from that field as she was nearly done her residency.

Parenthood in the early adult years is like being a freshman in high school. You learn through initiation what you will have to do and do without. Despite having gestational diabetes with the previous pregnancy, it was not identified with this pregnancy. The necessary testing had been done and she was instructed "there is no concern - no gestational diabetes." Weeks and months passed.

His sister knew he was on his way. His older brother couldn't wait. Of gentle-spirit and inviting to all infants, his preschool-aged older brother was certain to be the most-present companion with Tommy in pictures and in fun. Mom and baby survived a car accident, bed rest, and the every day stress of pregnancy. During a regular check up a week before scheduled induction Jim's wife mentioned a feeling of unease to her doctor, specifically that the baby wasn't moving as much. Prudently, the doctor put the Doppler right on her belly and a heartbeat came through. Liz laughed at her insecurity and followed the physician's confidence. Still, something seemed amiss.

Sent home after hearing a solid heartbeat and scheduled to deliver in just a couple of days, Mom struggled through the evening. Her head ached from the confusion of what appeared to be unsubstantiated worry and assumed dramatics. The house was full and active on a weeknight. The phone was ringing. The news was on. The family needed dinner. All she wanted to do was sleep. It would be a respite and safe haven for mother with child. Liz marched quietly through her struggle taking care of everyone else. Finally with the kids tucked away for the night, Tommy and his mom laid down. They would need each other's strength through the next day.

Maternal instinct woke her. Fear enveloped the morning routine of breakfast, tending to the family dog, dressing the kids and sending them off to school. Liz never looked at the calendar. She dropped her son at preschool and drove straight to the hospital. Apologetically she asked the staff, " I am so sorry to bother you. I was just here last night but please can you check me. I am not feeling my baby move."

The Doppler was silent. Liz's third grade daughter had the day off from school. She was assigned to a stool next to the ultra sound technician. The room fell dark and artificially silent. He would always be hers alone. Gray faded over mom's world. The doctor pushed hard and repeatedly on her belly. Phones were dialed. Nurses rushed in and out. The big sister stared unable to find the words or the comprehension. Mom's heart was breaking. People and equipment swirled around her. Tommy was quiet.

It would have an affect on Jim. Jim had a leg up on us in terms of what would happen in a lawsuit. Unfortunately now, I knew where he was headed in grief. Yet there was nothing I could do. I didn't "check in" for a long time. The notes and communications sent to the lawyer's office were to extend sympathies and offer comfort. Hopefully, he felt he could take a break. These were good people. How could he be hit with the same sour taste of life? All that stuff I wrote and poured out in my grief he had somewhere. I hoped now he hadn't actually read any of it.

Privy to the insider knowledge of medical practice and legalities, Jim would not pursue legal noise. With a silent dignity, they moved on with grace. Tommy would not have annual memorial fundraisers. Tommy would not have a foundation in his name. Tommy has a box, a teddy bear and a tattoo. Tommy will always have two parents, three sisters and one big brother. They will always have Tommy.

Perhaps the worst thing Jim did for my son's case was truly care. I doubt he could have done anything else. So, at this deposition, it was not just a lawyer and client. We had both just welcomed a new life into each of our families. We knew the bittersweet fortune of a subsequent child after burying a baby.

As I read Kochilas's deposition a month after it was given, I kept stopping and re-reading. It was an honest and forthcoming testimony. Certainly not what was expected from someone who appeared to be running away.

"Do you have a recollection of the treatment and care of James Mannix postoperatively on October 4, 2001 when you first arrived?" Jim queried.

Kochilas answered, "Yes, Dr. Raphaely gave me the sign out on patients including, James Mannix. He told me he was operated on earlier in the day and was removed from the mechanical ventilator support about one, one and a half hours before I arrived, and we reviewed the patient's nursing sheet that you have in front of you."

The conversation flowed as most other depositions did. Logistics and groundwork were laid. Point by point. Lab value by lab value. Minute by minute. His arrival that unfortunate evening was a bit delayed as he was arriving from his laboratory an hour away. It was not a normal schedule for him to work on a Thursday evening either. He agreed to switch his Friday evening shift for another's Thursday.

During rounds, James's tendency to retain carbon dioxide and his issue with hypoventilation was discussed. There was discussion on an appropriately comfortable range of oxygenation for a postoperative patient such as James.

"For a patient that is otherwise doing well, I would go like 55 up to 80. Normal values in a newborn they're like 60 over 80, but it's not unusual after an operation to have some ventilation profusion mismatches," Kochilas explained. "At 4:30 there's a gas that reads 7.39, 58.9, and then 64 the O2."

Jim asked, "It looks like the last saturation by Pulse oximetry reading was at 4:00 or 4:10 time period. I don't see any afterwards until it looks like 19:40 or so. Any idea why there is no recording in those spaces?"

"No."

Jim pressed, "Is that something that would typically be recorded?"

A definitive, "Yes." He went on to say he would normally consider reintubating a child such as James when evaluating his progress and care. Then he either was quite honest or slipped thinking it would help his defense. Jim asked if he had been in the unit and involved in James's care between sign out and James's arrest.

"I was initially in the unit. At the time of the arrest, I was not in the unit."

"Where were you?"
"I had just stepped out of the hospital and I was bringing dinner."

"Do you recall where you went for dinner?"

"Yes. Well, I didn't go for dinner. I was just picking up food."

"Was it like a pizza place, a take-out place or something?"

"A take-out place."

"Do you know about what time it was that you left?"

"I don't know. I don't remember the exact time, but I know that it was during this time the event happened."

"Where did you go?" Jim pushed.

"I don't remember the name. It's just across the - what is the name? I mean there is a main street very close to the hospital. So, I remember that when I was called, I was back in less than five minutes, which could be – you could be in a distant place in the hospital and that would be about the time you would get back." Kochilas explained.

I remembered it took five minutes to get from the main entrance to the CICU. So, I perceived that there was no way that he could also return from a restaurant to James's bedside in five minutes. The hospital was set off the main road, and part of acres of beautifully landscaped estate, once through the gated entrance, it took another three minutes to find a parking spot.

It was a quick exchange between defendant and opposing counsel, as each realized the weight of this play. Jim was starting to envision his battle. This was a soft spot for the defense without a doubt. Attending physicians are presumed by the general public to be in presence and attending their patients. Certainly not getting dinner. Jim had a point, Why not have an orderly get the take out?

"When you arrived at the hospital was CPR in progress?"

"Yes." There were no physicians present.

As the doctor continued revealing his experience that night with James, light was being shed on James's experience too. The doctor had to open James's chest for two reasons: "One to make sure that you don't have tamponade becuase that's the only way to view the heart. The second thing is to do direct cardiac massage because it can be more effective from outside. The third is if we needed to go on bypass, you have done the first steps and will save some time."

Kochilas continued to help turn over a significant boulder in trying to find what happened to James.

Even after the boulder was removed something was missing. Kochilas acknowledged reviewing telemetry monitor tracings after the event. He wanted to see if they would help in explaining what happened. Why did James arrest?

I would never see this part of my son's life – either in real time or on paper. My attorney would be refused the opportunity and any expert he could ask would not be able to see them. In deposition and again at trial all the medically trained witnesses testified that this piece of James's medical records would be most helpful in explaining to the jury what happened to James. The healthcare team did not save the tracings. Hospital risk managers did not furnish them. Dr. Kochilas discussed the case with others to try and learn what had happened. Only the following morning did an anesthesiologist present during the surgery mention issues with elevated pulmonary pressure. It unfortunately was not a piece of information discussed at hand-off. Per his own testimony, the compassionate doctor would have liked to have that piece of information when James was entrusted to his care.

Fall was fast approaching. Tommy was in mind as September approached. There would be little time to worry. There was very little warning when Jim's dad died a week before Tommy's first birthday/anniversary. Mr. Beasley was not my lead attorney but I liked knowing he was there. He reminded me of my dad. They were born the same year. They both lied about their age to serve in World War II. I never saw the tough side that made him well known and successful. I just remembered how much I appreciated someone like my dad acknowledging the enormity of James's loss without qualification. Like a caring patriarch, he had gently taken me by the hand as a partner in a dance from the first phone call, escorted me briefly in a waltz and, after asking my permission, passed my hand to a capable partner. I could barely fathom how momentous this loss would be to his son. It would have been appropriate to for Jim ease up on work. However, the pace was picking up in James's case.

There was a viewing, a funeral, an Irish wake and Tommy's birthday all the same week. Jim was present, busy and focused. Just a couple weeks later, I was deposed on the third anniversary of James's funeral. It was tough. For nearly eight hours defense counsel grilled me on everything from where my kids went to school to how adept I was on the computer. I felt stupid and ignorant. How could I possibly have believed there were no risks in surgery? It was the longest of all the depositions in James's case. I have no medical training. All the jargon and information I understand now came as a direct result of the lawsuit. I dressed professionally and respectfully and tried to be comfortable. I was not. I felt like this was my chance to tell James's story. The paralegal was quick to remind me it was not. Not yet. In deposition the defense attorneys focused on what I did and did not do before James was born. They asked things about the new child and the surviving siblings.

There were many insignificant questions and answers. Most stunning and even crushing at times was the concentration on how I did or did not appropriately interview my newborn child's prospective physicians. I remember having confidence in the system: confidence in The Joint Commission accreditation, confidence in insurance and government oversight, confidence that I did not have the prescribed knowledge to understand everything.

At my deposition, Norwood's attorney took the lead in questioning me. She asked, "Before I move onto another topic I just want to make sure you've told me all you can remember today about Dr. Norwood. Okay so I assume that when you pointed down to the middle of your chest and called it a sternum, that's a word that you have learned since the time you talked to Dr. Norwood correct?"

I calmly replied," That's correct."

"But what he did during that conversation was point to his chest?" the attorney clarified.

"Yes."

She continued with an air of either disbelief or pure superiority, "And draw kind of a line down through the middle of the chest indicating that he would be splitting the sternum or cutting open the sternum; is that correct?"

Whether she believed me or not, agreed with how I handled it or not, I had to reply honestly as I was under oath and I had nothing to hide, "I did not know at that time what he was referring to." During that meeting the word "sternum" was never used. I would not have known to use it to even ask.

She pushed, "Did you ask him?"

"No. No."

And she went even farther in judgment, "so your recollection is you asked him what he would be doing and he kind of made a line down through the center of his chest, and that's where you left it?"

"Yes," my heart and my shoulders sank. I could not hide the defeat. If I had not "just left it" perhaps things would be different.

"And when you asked him about anesthesia, he told you that it would be general anesthesia, correct?"

"Right." This surgeoun had not reviewed the referring doctor's notes. Norwood said it himself as he threw a file on his desk while leaning back on a roomy, high-backed leather chair, "I would concur with whatever Dr. Bhat said."

Bhat had said we would "not be talking open heart surgery here." When a world-renowned surgeon wants to talk a little bit, you let him. Perhaps, it was that Catholic school education or my middle class awe. Either way, I was trained well to give deference to anyone wearing a white lab coat who had a large framed parchment hung on the wall above his head. Degrees meant knowledge and integrity. I realized then that experience as a plaintiff was giving me an education you can't that can't be found in ivory halls.

The following day, I traveled back to Center City for Norwood's deposition. Relieved after the previous day's workday long deposition, today's events were to be redeeming. I was alone as Michael was unable to get away from work. I would definitely be relying on Jim today. It was a good thing we were at The Beasley Building for this one. We sat in the downstairs boardroom which was much more elegant than the drab, dirty, untended attorney's office from my deposition. The chairs were more comfortable, the surroundings familiar and reassuring. We walked into the room from the rear entrance. Across the table sat a lawyer that was becoming a regular fixture for the defense and two others that showed themselves only sporadically. I knew how much they had riding on one of their defendant's testimony by how many showed up to listen. There were five lawyers and one paralegal in the room for Norwood's deposition. This guy had created his own economy with several professionals now relying on him for vacations and tuition payments.

He was as I remembered – much taller than I, a white man with some girth, a deep voice to carry the weight, and gray on top to complete the stereotypical image. As he looked at me sheepishly, he had to brush his hair off his face. His tie was a bit rumpled and not tied all together tight. He appeared insecure.

I turned to Jim and shared, "I feel sorry for him."

"Don't." Jim replied succinctly and making firm eye contact.

It was an awkward reunion. Just like meeting the hero quarterback that led your high school football team to a championship season. Long after the ten-year reunion, the former star is wearing a sanitation worker uniform and a beer belly. I knew I shouldn't feel bad for the guy, for it was his own decisions that led to his failure. And his decisions, not mine, that led to my sweet baby James's traumatic death. In the years since my son's fateful meeting with this surgeon, there was information discovered about who he was and what he had been doing.

In October 2000, Norwood was found negligent and responsible in the care of a six month old boy who had come to him for a repair of coarctation of the aorta. The care was delivered at a big city children's hospital in the early 90's. The little boy, Stephen, had presented with a hole in his heart. Hearing someone has a hole in their heart is alarming. However, many VSDs close or shrink on their own. Surgery was not the first option given. Stephen's mom and dad consented to a repair of the Coarct through a left thoracotomy. The hole was not to be addressed in anyway. With the guide of their cardiologist, they would wait to see if it closed on its own. I remembered this story and that James did not have a hole in his heart.

When Norwood began surgery on little Stephen, his eyes were taped shut. He was placed on a sterile, metal table and administered general anesthesia. He was cooled rapidly to 15 degrees Fahrenheit. His heart was stopped and a machine was utilized for his circulation while Norwood made an incision down the middle of the baby's chest. In addition to repairing the coarctation, Norwood closed the hole in his heart. In recovery, Stephen exhibited seizures and suffered an "event." Stephen went home eventually, but was severely brain-damaged. He was wheeled into a courtroom in October 2000. Though he could not speak or walk on his own, he smiled and reacted to his father's voice. He is a beautiful child.

Stephen's mother and father face the daily challenges of a severely disabled child. After the case had gone to the jury, they were offered another settlement. To ensure care of their child, they accepted the large sum. Minutes later, the jury returned a verdict of fifty-five million dollars for the plaintiffs. It was the largest medical malpractice award in Pennsylvania history. Though they had already agreed to a maximum amount that was much less than the jury knew the family needed, it was a clear loss for the defense. This case was highlighted in "Philadelphia" magazine as the medical malpractice "crisis" gained momentum in the media during 2001. The article was published in its September 2001 issue.

James did not have a hole in his heart. James only had a coarctation. He was born with a discrete coarctation as shown by echocardiogram and diagnosed by Norwood's own associates. Unfortunately, James's course was similar in many ways to Stephen's. Within a week of the surgery he had performed, Norwood's patient was brain damaged and his mom was mad. Instead of speaking to me, he stayed as far away as possible and made decisions that in the end would be to the surgeon's benefit. Not the patient's. Not even his associates'.

My daily presence at James's side was not as commonplace as I would have expected among the other CICU patients. I was fortunate in having family nearby that was able and willing to stay with my older children while I kept vigil in the hospital. Also it was good fortune that Michael had a steady job with flexibility and compassionate management. In hindsight, my presence threatened the doctor and as such ultimately threatened this helpless baby's life.

On a feeble attempt to get specifics from the nursing staff as to Norwood's reaction the morning after his arrest, a nurse shared, "oh, he was mad. He was REALLY mad." The neglect shown by his subordinates for his masterful operation really ticked him off. From the morning of the 5th, Norwood continued to defer us to Raphaely with every question, concern and inquiry we brought him. It was as if, Raphaely screwed this up, he will have to fix it. Norwood turned away from my son and from us. It took me the following years to learn what Norwood had learned in the previous years. He could be held liable for his actions. From his attire and identifying badges to his words and actions, all could be questioned and documented. After the initial event, there was little contact with Norwood despite a daily attempt from my husband or I. After the surgery on the 12th Norwood not only did not avail himself, he removed all scrubs and hospital identification before venturing out to patients and families.

While James was alive the coarctation was always mentioned as "discrete." This description of a coarctation identifies it as one that is more manageable. Much later, after the "sudden event," the term "Hypoplastic" appeared. This was a new, more clinical term. Hypoplastic meant it would have been a bit more difficult to manage. Jim asked Norwood about the discrepancy, "Do you recall reading anywhere in the chart, whether radiology reports, any type of imaging reports or any notes from the cardiologist preoperatively that called James's aortic arch Hypoplastic?"

"You mean using specifically the term Hypoplastic? I don't recall," Norwood replied in deposition. Norwood acknowledged moments earlier, "I'm not an echocardiographer, an imager with magnetic resonance imaging. I relied on, as usual, cardiologists to bring forth the kind of diagnostic information that would provide a road map for surgery."

This had to be explored further, "Does anything on that sheet or any other sheet that you have seen provide support for the position that there was a Hypoplastic arch preoperatively?"

"It says – a discrete coarctation of the aorta at the isthmus is appreciated with the isthmus narrowing to 2.2 millimeters. Transverse aortic arch is 3.9 millimeters. That's what it says," Norwood documented. It was a highly technical discourse. In time, I would research all these terms. Jim and Norwood were discussing the position of the narrowing of James' aorta as well as how thin the narrowing was.

"The numbers you just read, the ascending aortic aorta of 4.3. the transverse aortic arch of 3.9, is that within the range of normal, or would you consider that to be abnormally low numbers in a patient such as James?" Jim asked.

The doctor reveled in this discussion. Clearly he knew baby hearts. He sat taller and was at ease as the conversation stayed on the technical specifics of pediatric cardiology. Straight answers were an anomaly. "One can have a spectrum of sizes that are – that don't just suddenly fall off and you say, ah-ha, this is now Hypoplastic. It's a spectrum. I would say 4.3 is on the small side for an ascending aorta in a full term baby. Does that in and of it self portend adverse physiological consequences? That size is going to be on the small side, but it probably will not for an ascending aorta. The isthmus measuring 2.2 millimeters is extremely small."

As I listened to the established physician, it was apparent that if this was all true then information had been withheld from me before James was even in any trouble. This information would have had a significant impact on the decisions for treatment, as well as the reaction to any adverse event during or after treatment. That is if I had been included in the decision making process. Jim and Norwood continued through a "laundry list of possible causes of James's cardiovascular collapse." As they went through the surgeon confidently declared "no" to all possibilities save ventilation. The answers became more hair-splitting. This was characteristic of all the defense depositions when it arrived at the area of James's postoperative ventilation and his "sudden event."

Jim tried to focus the physician, "All I was getting at-in this process, you were describing I think two answers ago - was the ability of the patient to breathe beyond the setting of the ventilator something that is considered in the extubation process, considered in the decision making process as to whether to extubate?"

"Yes," Norwood admitted. "One physically observes the quantity and quality of respiratory movements that the individual is having outside of the influence of machinery, the mechanical ventilation itself."

"Why is it important in a patient such as James from the extubation process to see what they're trying to breathe above and beyond the ventilator settings?"

"Patients do have to breathe," the surgeon instructed. "As you turn down the mechanical ventilatory support, and if there is absolutely no effort from the child, then you have to start thinking of other things. I mean, all babies that are awake enough to have muscular tone enough to breathe will breathe as you turn the ventilatory support down. You don't turn it to zero. You turn it to some very low number, which is essentially a number of breaths to overcome the smaller size of the endotracheal tube that is necessarily smaller than the trachea so the baby is not breathing through a straw, so to speak. So, generally wean to five, six, seven IMV. If the baby is vigorous and breathing beyond that number, through experience, will tell you that when you take the tube out, the baby will continue to breathe in satisfactory fashion, generally at the same rate, maybe changing somewhat either up or down with the tube no longer in place." Norwood was describing the ventilator system James was on after his surgery. It was one that would allow the patient to breathe above the amount of breaths per minutes the machine would do for the patient. He also confirmed no provider should take a baby off this mechanical support until the baby shows he or she is breathing independently of it. James was not there. More time would have helped him. Proper placement of the breathing tube may have helped as well.

Jim asked, "When you were trying to figure out what happened to James, did you folks either individually or collectively, determine whether James's breathing was beyond the settings on the ventilator?"

"I personally wasn't there, so I can't answer that question with any direct information." Norwood referred us back to Raphaely's testimony, among others, which concluded that James never breathed above the ventilator settings.

After Norwood's deposition I allowed Jim to remove him from the case. Jim had kept me abreast with the direction the case needed to take to be argued in court so a jury could understand at least one of the several points of negligence. James's case was complex. There was a multitude of egregious, preventable errors: each one growing more severe from the previous. How could a jury understand that a child born with a physical anomaly is still viable? Despite all the best in medical advances, generally the public associates a need of medical treatment to a life less valued. Despite the appropriateness and quality of the care received, if one dies from it or the lack of it, hey – that's okay. Without it death would be imminent anyway. That is often just not the case.

What if I had not had proper prenatal care?

James coarctation would not have been found before he was born, I would not have seen or discussed any of the possibilities. I would have brought James home. Within a few days James would have been showing signs of cardiac distress. He would have started sweating during feeding. He would have been sleeping a great deal more than the normal newborn. There would have been two possibilities.

In my first fantasy, I wouldn't have been alarmed enough to act. He would have slept in his own bassinette. Worn many of the clothes purchased for him. His sisters and brothers would have had the chance to hold him and know him. He would have met the neighbors. He would have received "Welcome Home" cards. He also could have suffered an arrest at home, 911 called and he could have died. Perhaps even in my arms. There would have been a larger community of support to share our grief and sadness. I may have been there for James in his final moments of life.

In the next dream, I would have been alarmed enough to act and would have brought him to the Children's Hospital of Philadelphia. We would have been given all treatment options. I would have chosen the least risky path, which is how I historically made all healthcare decisions regarding my children. He could have made it. He would have been called a miracle.

Yes, James needed medical attention. He didn't require it until after the medical team had touched him. The health system made him sicker. Without the broken system, James, if he was destined to die as a newborn, would have died within the arms of his mother. His life experience would have been more worth living. As it was, patients in this CIC U were denied much touch from loved ones or clinicians. In those hours after surgery where his father and mother were denied access to him, the clinicians allowed needles and machine to touch him with a schedule. Several blood gases screamed for James to be re-offered help in breathing while his body was adjusting that Thursday afternoon and evening. He was left to his own devices. He gasped and he tried desperately to suck in the oxygen his new body needed.

Jim had begun to visualize an argument and focus of the suit to bring ease of clarity. That was a hard puzzle piece for me to place. Within minutes of completing deposition in our law firm's office, Jim was on the move. I heard the directive, "Stand here. You can see from here." From the top of the mahogany stairs, I quietly watched below as Norwood was served with papers on the newest complaint. Some other family was struggling. I still didn't understand the subtleties and complexities of the law. This attorney had a greater knowledge, ability, and bravado to find the best way through an endlessly shifting maze. I was a sad mom in need of an advocate. Preventable medical error is such an unpopular way to die.

It had been a long morning coupled with the exhausting previous day. There was no way to appreciate the toll straddling my emotions was taking. It was good to have someone fighting for my son's life and my pain. It was arriving back home to one less bed, one less mouth to feed and unsure of when I would hear his name again that was unbearable. I would turn to a Reese's Big Cup again. There was nowhere else to go. I was turning into a Big Cup too.

When my dad died, it was clear I would have to ascertain under varying circumstances how to act. It would depend on who was there, where we were, what was happening, and even what time of year it was. At twelve I had just started to understand I had my own identity. I would need to figure out with each of my surviving children what they each individually needed. One child needed to not talk about it. One child needed to talk about it all the time. One child needed to act like it didn't even happen. Sometimes, I needed to talk about it. Other times, I needed to push it so far out of my mind it was more a dream than reality. And often, I just couldn't even say his name as much as I needed to hear it. What I needed never matched with the child I was with at the time. I just knew I needed them. I was grateful they were here. It was so sad they would know senseless tragedy so early in their own lives. I tried for normalcy. Returning from two days of depositions was not normal. When the humdrum of homework help, taxiing middle schoolers, and getting laundry done hit, my patience was not even. My words were often poorly chosen. My kids always forgave me.

I still look at his living peers with awe, wonder and heavy longing. I can now recognize other grieving parents by that look. Like the dad in the store just down the aisle who watched and listened to my daughter as she talked descriptively of rather inane things that are terribly important to an eight year old. The challenge is how to approach that grieving parent that I have never met. Perhaps starting with "how old was your child?" Or maybe just "Do you have any kids?" Yet, I am keenly aware of the strain those series of words can put on a parent raw with grief. "Do I tell this person?" "Is it worth getting into, I may never see this person again?" I end up remembering my own rawness and have only once "put myself out there" for another. There are no easy answers. As such there is no easy way to accept that you misplaced trust.

How sorry I am. How terribly sorry.

I have to keep living. Keep moving. Keep laughing. In time things will roll off your back little by little. Little things can roll off much easier than larger ones. The burden becomes a bit lighter. People may not know what to say but their presence is priceless.

Be gentle on yourself. There is no time limit here.

Bedside nurses are referred to as on the front line and direct caregivers in quality and safety discussions – for good reason. If best practices and how to implement doesn't reach the bedside nurses, the months of research, planning, evaluation and training done by administrators, risk managers and invested consumers is lost one patient at a time.

Having a sister as a student nurse wasn't pleasant for me around the Sunday dinner table. The talk of blood, guts, and human excrement was more than I could stomach. Working with young children, I had always had my full of bodily fluids that escaped on their own. Voluntarily going beyond the skin was gross. Despite the different levels of tolerance, the nurse's abilities, dedications, and duties were worthy of respect and awe. So, hearing some of her patient stories were reminders to stay healthy but be grateful for those willing to care for me if I got sick. I kept this in mind when I sat next to James's bed in 2001. The nurses had patients beyond my own and families beyond the hospital. Ray was one of James's primary nurses. It was great to see my son being cared for a male nurse. He was recently married without any children of his own, but he had a big dog.

I didn't realize how little he could actually care for a pediatric cardiac patient post-surgery until over three years after James's death. What is rarely included in depositions is the time taken by the deposed to answer each question. The start and end time are recorded. Together with the amount of information gathered in that time period, some configuration to the rhythm of the questioning can be assessed. It certainly can't do it justice like being there.

Ray was stymied during most of his deposition. His began at 10:31 in the morning and was completed by 11:13. It was a brief deposition made longer by extensive periods of silence as everyone waited for him to answer even simple inquiries.

Trying to understand what his duties were Jim asked, "what was your duty in the cardiac intensive care unit? What did you do? What was your job title?"

"Registered nurse."

"Or responsibility?" Jim clarified.

"That's two different things."

"Your title was a nurse, an RN?"

"Yes."

"What are your responsibilities?"

We waited for a response. Eventually he offered, "I think that's a bit broad to ask. I have many responsibilities."

Patiently and with respect, Jim clarified, "You're not operating, so one of your responsibilities is not to do surgery. What does an RN do in the cardiac care unit at Nemours in the October of '01 time period?"

Ray had to repeat the question, "What do I do? I guess as the bedside nurse I'm responsible for recording vital signs as ordered, and assessing the patient at each time frame."

Perhaps the question wasn't as simple as it sounded. Perhaps, it is appropriate that he thought before he spoke. Working with preschoolers, I know the research. A four year old needs at least 30 seconds to hear the question or directive, assimilate and then understand enough to respond appropriately. Good teaching practices in early childhood education include a great deal of patience. It was unexpected to see this needed in a specialty intensive care unit nurse. Jim had to reorganize and simplify his questions time and time again.

Jim took him through James's course on the fateful Thursday afternoon and early evening. Again the breathing rate changes and blood gases were addressed. Most of Ray's replies were, "I don't remember" or "I don't recall" or "I cannot answer that." It got so tough for the nurse he eventually just stopped answering.

Jim was investigating the medications given and the participation of physicians and physician's assistants. "This morphine, was that a continuous drip or just a one hit thing?"

"One hit," Ray answered.

"Do you have any idea how long that effect lasts?"

"Off the top of my head, no."

"Can you tell us whether the respiratory rate was written before or after you got the morphine, the respiratory rate of 42?"

Time passed. He took a look at the chart in front of him. He looked over at Jim again. Then back to the chart. And then, "It appears to be before the morphine."

"Any understanding as to why his breathing [breaths per minute] went from 80 down to 42 between the 18:00 block and the 19:00 block?"

Again, time was passing. Ray was reviewing the chart. He was looking at Jim. Eventually, "No, I do not."

"Did you bring these changes in respirations from 15:00 being at 20, 16:00 being 44, 17:00 being at 60, 18:00 being at 80, and then 19:00 being at 42 to a physician, a physician's assistant, or a nurse practitioner at 19:00 when you wrote the 42?"

"I do not recall." Ray was very uncomfortable and had no support in the lawyer sitting next to him. Ray never received an opportunity to express what this event meant to him or how it affected his life. Ray seemed fearful.

Jim wondered, "Would your standard practice have been to alert one of these healthcare providers, physician, physician assistant, or nurse practitioner about the changes in respiration?"

He changed his position in his seat and slowly answered, "Yes."

"Other than you monitoring James, how did it work generally with the physicians or physicians assistants or nurse practitioners coming into the unit? Were they always kind of there floating around and seeing what was going on with the patient in addition to you doing that?"

"I do not recall." He was wearing a badge that indicated, and he verified, he still worked there.

So, Jim tried again, gently and with encouragement, "Well, just generally the way it works there in the cardiac intensive care unit, is it mostly the nurses there are keeping track and they call the docs or the nurse practitioners or the physician's assistant if there's an issue, or are the physicians, physician's assistants, or nurse practitioners kind of floating through the unit as well?"

We waited. Jim looked across the table patiently. I did the same. I looked back at Jim a few times to see what else he might do as the minutes clocked by. He kept a calm and steady gaze on the deposed. There was still another nurse to be deposed so this would need to be encouraged along.

There was never an answer. As a matter of record, the deposition reads "There was no response."

Though it was certainly familiar and we were back at the same hospital for this deposition, the practice of not answering was not creating a feeling of security. It was again strengthening my resolve. Jim went on with a few more questions and continued to get much the same delayed responses if any. More, "I don't recall." And "I don't remember." But Jim went ahead and tried one last time, "You were involved in his care. Can you tell me generally what you remember about your involvement in his care on those subsequent dates?"

"I think the only thing I recall is that he expired on the day I was taking care of him."

That would be hard to forget. I remember this fellow like crystal. The day after James's crash, he came to me and asked, "What happened? When I left, James was fine. He was doing great."

And on the day he died, this guy asked if I wanted a picture of my son. I said NO. I had no interest in a picture of him so mutilated and dead. He must have quickly forgotten that request when he was clicking the Polaroid over a dead newborn baby boy.

Again, I could see the sun shining outside of the hospital window. Inside the gray storm clouds were rolling again. The collection of information I had uncovered under this giant rock was not expected three years after the event. Attending the nurse's deposition was out of an established habit. There was discussion to not attend. Jim encouraged us. Arrangements to take off work, find sitters, benign explanations to our growing more curious children were all made. There I sat, dumbfounded and amazed at my own stupidity.

I thought I surely knew everything there was to understand from the previous meetings with physicians and experts. Nurse Ray's deposition was revealing for his inability to think, understand, and coherently communicate his job and responsibilities to another adult. Just before him was a nurse who seemed unwilling or unable to feel compassion. This was not the picture of nursing my sister had left imprinted.

The most disturbing testimony came from the same nurse that expressed to me my son's beauty the night of his birth. As impressive as he was to her that night, the eventual course his treatment took was evidently easy to forget.

Again, same room, same place, same lawyer asking many foundation questions. The enormity of my involvement never was lessened. Each and every deposition, there was appreciation and awe. Not once were we asked for money or reimbursement for the time and preparations he incurred. It was an unknown as to whether there would be any financial recovery. His concern for that was second to recovering a slice of justice for my son and I. He asked questions he knew I had regardless of their impact on any future courtroom argument or motion.

Jim started searching for established policies, procedures, protocols present in the cardiac intensive care unit in the October 2001 time frame. He wanted to know about reporting lab values, re-intubating patients, an attending physician's physical location and availability, the role of a nurse practitioner, and emergency codes. As usual, the deposed denied knowing or remembering any. Quite opposite of her colleague, this nurse was leaning forward on the table across from us and shared her answers in a commanding demeanor, without hesitations.

She began with her first entry into James's flowchart – the papers that were utilized by the nurse and physicians to keep track of everything as it was happening to my son under their care.

"At 19:30 the baby awoke, heart rate decreased, requiring hand ventilation to bring the heart rate back up with a mask, and medications were given to achieve that goal." She was ready. Her bedside manner and sense of empathy for a patient had been checked at the door.

Jim slowed her down to go left from right, point to point.

"My initial heart rate was 138 and it had changed by the time I finished writing to 107. I have an arrow indicating that it was beginning to decrease."

"At that point what did you do?" Jim asked.

"At that point according this note when the baby awoke with the heart rate decreasing, even though I don't have written here, called for assistance, that's standard. I called for assistance, that being the nurses that were there with me. And again I do not know who they were, I do not remember who they were as well as the nurse practitioner."

I should have interrupted and congratulated her for that voluntary admission.

Jim pressed on:

Q: "So do you have any recollection of this baby awaking and you calling for assistance and all that?"

A: "Other than what I see written here and that we reviewed on Monday, no, I do not remember the event or baby."

Q: "Does this chart evidence the fact that you were involved in his case the whole night?'

A: "Yes," the nurse answered to Jim's inquiry.

Q: "When you went through this did you have an understanding as to what happened to him that evening?"

A: "At the time it was occurring, certainly. And in reviewing afterwards, I can certainly track as to our actions to correct the situation that we were seeing."

Q: "And what is it that happened to him?" Jim asked.

Having difficulty refraining from being annoyed, she answered, "Again as I just said, he awoke, his heart rate decreased, he was having an episode where he was not tolerating being awake is what I'm gathering from this. Again, my brief notations here are dealing with our interventions."

Ignoring her deprecation, the lawyer continued, "What are some of the interventions that you did?"

"Hand ventilating with a mask and giving medications." She went to add that she administered atropine, bicarbonate, and calcium.

"Aren't they part of a code type treatment?"

"Yes."

"So this baby arrested?"

Her caution kept in check. "I could not tell you exactly what happened again because I don't recall. I'm only going by what is here," she said.

In agreement Jim said, "That's what I'm trying to understand. Did you ever come to learn that they had to do open heart massage and all that on him?"

"Certainly."

"Where did that occur based on your understanding of this?"

"At the bedside," she answered without hesitation.

"And it's your testimony that you have no recollection of that at all?"

It was necessary for her to explain. "Only by reading this do I recall that it happened. I don't recall specifically the baby. I can read and recall that I read the notes and I can understand what I've written and why I've given it, but that's the extent of my memory," she said.

That review meeting on Monday must have included some elements of coaching. She was a quick study.

It was certainly safer for the objective party to speak, "Let me try to understand something then. We have a baby who is having open heart massage in a cardiac intensive care unit, and it's your testimony that you don't remember it?" Jim asked.

"Yes."

"Is that a typical thing that happens all the time and that's why the memory is blurred?"

"I can't say that it happens all the time, " she coolly replied.

The discussion returned to the course of events as closely as could be followed with the records produced. "So how do we know these times are reliable?" Jim asked.

She answered, "Other than the fact that that's what I wrote, you don't."

She continued, "Generally, in my practice, strictly for preference since I don't generally like people writing on my flow sheet because I want to understand it, also helps me to review what's going on for me to write it down. Generally, what I have people do, people helping me, again, I couldn't tell you specifically who it was, but it would be an RN, is usually writing this down making notations with times that they're writing down vital signs, doing actions, keeping a record. While I'm drawing up and giving medications, they're doing the writing portion on another piece of paper. And then I transcribe it onto the flow sheet, make sense of, unscramble it, etc."

"Is it a piece of paper incorporated into the chart?"

"No," the nurse replied.
"What do they do with that piece of paper?"

"Once all the data has been transferred over here, it's thrown out because it's not an official piece of paper."

To clarify Jim inquired, "So all things being equal, there would have been another piece of paper where another nurse would have been a recorder if you will and then that data would have been later put into the chart by you?"

"Correct."

"And then that sheet gets trashed?"

"Correct."

Jim marched on through the arrest with the nurse acknowledging a low potassium level could cause an arrhythmia, that my son's blood gases were unbalanced, that the breathing tube had been placed and repositioned, his pH was getting worse, his chest was being opened and his slight rise in pulsatile flow was a result of direct cardiac massage.

"Okay. And some medications were given, I assume?"

"Yes."

"What was given?" Jim asked.

"Again, epinephrine (to increase the heart rate), was given in two separate doses, and we also gave a paralytic - pancuronium."

"Why would you paralyze him?"

"At this point, there must have been movement. The surgeon felt that it was safer to paralyze him because as we're in the chest, you don't want the baby to move and create potential problems."

My heart stopped. My breathing was shallow. My blood had slowed. This was all too easy to envision. Hearing repeatedly that he had cried right before his "event" will always be a struggle. Now, he was also moving while they cracked open his chest, spread his breastbone for the second time in one day, maneuvered inside his tiny body with all sorts of hands and instruments. He was administered a paralytic but never given any painkillers.

Jim asked, "Any idea why he would be moving?"

She didn't skip a beat, "Because he was awake."

Jim kept moving. I was back in 2001 trying to save my son. Their voices became muddled background noise while I worked to stay calm. No wonder he died. Absent a painkiller yet paralyzed for open heart and direct cardiac massage, this was a horror movie James was born into. I, though not voluntarily, deserted the discussion to survive what had already happened.

When I came to, Jim had the nurse reading from the flow sheet, "Let me just stop you there. You said mid-code. Did somebody call a code for this?"

"No" the nurse replied. "That's strictly the word I chose to use."

"So nobody pulled the alarm and –"
"No we don't do that."

"How do people know to come help?"

"We internalize."

She went on to explain the training received upon hire within the Nemours Cardiac Center, they would prefer to keep such an event internalized and utilize their own doctors and nurses, nurse practitioners and respiratory therapists. The conversation continued. Family and the priest were mentioned. Then again, I was reminded as they came close to the end of the chart of that disastrous evening, the nurse was reading her notes, "Does occasionally twitch and open eyes for stimulation, paralytics given as noted."

"What does that mean, he's waking up again?"

"Yes."

"In addition to being paralyzed, can you tell us whether there were any medicines to control pain, any opiates anything like that that were given?"

"I don't see any that were given, no. Parents were still at the bedside."

They just kept paralyzing him. How could he possibly self-soothe if he couldn't move but could still feel the pain? That's like being set on fire and not being able to move.

As we left the hospital after this trifecta of nurses depositions, the sun was warm and the sky was a brilliant blue. Jim was kind and genuine in his words. He just kept saying he was sorry and asked if we needed anything. To survive meant a visit to the cemetery on the way home, where more apologies would blanket the grave. Eating too much of something would be my feeble attempt to forget and remember all at the same time. Drinking would have been a more attractive vice, leaving its slaves with slighter builds. Too bad I hadn't picked that one up. I would need something before the kids got home. This was tough.

A great deal happened to my son that night. Anyone could have told me over the remaining nine days of his life or during the follow up meeting a month after his death. I kept asking, "What happened?" No one would answer me. Some was being discovered through the justice system. There would be even more revealed in the courtroom.

*"Our lives begin to end the day we become
silent about things that matter."*

Martin Luther King

October 2, 2005

It was a Sunday early afternoon and we were in the city in the grand old refurbished church that housed our well-known lawyers. Something was missing this time. Jim's dad was gone. The old guy who was so gentle and kind to me, despite his reputation of being a razor sharp attorney, had died in the previous year. His presence surrounded us. The law books of the library we sat in were screaming to be read. I had entertained the idea of going to law school or nursing school after this case closed. I felt like I was gawking at the enormity of the volumes of law and legal cases surrounding me. I had grown an affection for mahogany as well. An instinct was cueing me to where this may be leading. While waiting for Jim as he ran from his office to another end of the building, I asked his associate, "How long have you been a lawyer?" She was a nurse first. At 40, she went back for a law degree with three kids at home. It could be done.

My energetic attorney sat down and though anxious to work he paused for a check in, "How you guys doing? Sorry that you have to be here today." It was a beautiful day. It was James's birthday. I asked if he had ever experienced or seen this irony before in any of his cases.

"No, this is a first. It may be to our advantage, as hard as it will be."

Understood.

There had been some quick, harried phone conversations at the end of the previous week and even on Saturday. The defense offered $750,000 and a confidentiality agreement to settle the case out of court. At some point in the previous years, the information I garnered about successful foundations was that a million was needed to start one. Right or wrong, it seemed the offer was not enough for an endowment to create a foundation that could help save others' from this dreadful fate. I really did not understand how not being able to talk about what happened to James would help. I could not live with myself if I allowed myself to be gagged with cash. That would do little good beyond blanketing the grave with more apologies and guilt.

Jim seemed to understand and was fine taking our case to court. I felt physically ill and terribly weak. A great deal had been given and sacrificed for my answers. There had to be a way to repay the attorney. I was worried I wouldn't be able to. Of course, he applied no pressure. If anything, he steered for the courtroom.

"So, Mary Ellen, have you thought about what you're going to wear tomorrow?"

Okay now this was a personal question. In four years I had shared my life's most difficult moments. He knew the inner workings of my family and my marriage. But what would I wear? How could I say I had been thinking hard on it and had worried about it as I had grown out of options. Michael had lost his job a few months previous. I was just outside of six weeks post-hysterectomy. There was no money for shopping and I had nothing to wear.

"No, not really."

The suggestion was something modest and not too flashy. It was time to make the right first impression on the jury pool. This was nerve wracking. Jim added, "I wouldn't mind at all if you cried."

I laughed out of nervousness. Jim perhaps had noticed over the years the defense mechanisms built up in me. Whereas our first phone conversations were marked with sniffles and deep breaths, now I was better at speaking straight logistics. In four years, I had lost what were once close family and friends. I had to move my family to a different neighborhood to escape judgments, both financial and personal. There was a mighty struggle to keep our family's practical needs met. I had learned to keep busy and to focus on the needs of another. Not thinking about the actual loss was the only way to maintain sanity. Jim knew how to cover the pain of loss to guard from vulnerability. The anniversaries of his son's and father's death had just passed days ago. He poured himself into his work and family. This month, I was that work. Now I didn't want to let him down.

I was being asked to be vulnerable again. Be vulnerable with people who I didn't know. Be vulnerable with people that my son knew well in his short life. Be vulnerable with the people that had initiated all the unnecessary pain in the first place. It was a full four years to learn how to compartmentalize the pain of the loss. Four years of re-learning, dependent on the situation and the company, to quickly ascertain actions and answers to questions like: "How many children do you have?" Now, it would be a test to see if not only was I able to keep the emotion at bay, when necessary, but also to lean on it. My skin had grown rather thick.

After a tempered celebration at the attorney's office and a depressing celebration at the cemetery- balloons and all, I gathered myself for cake and song with his siblings. I had to act like such a post-mortem party was normal. I knew it wasn't. That night I couldn't sleep. My heart kept reminding my head of all that had been lost. My baby died and I gained a law firm, yet lost a lawyer. My baby died and I gained a lawsuit, but lost the respect of friends and family. My baby died and I gained a lot of weight, lost much of it, and gained it back. No matter what happened, my baby would still be dead. How could I ever hold onto anything?

Strategically, my testimony would be called first or last. I would need to be ready.

I prayed. God help me. God, guide Jim, too. In the previous four years, he had become my voice. I had grown to have more faith in this guy a year older than me than in the religion I grew up with. Jim had given James a voice.

October 3, 2005

The courthouse was very modern. Long lines preceded
the metal detectors. Postings abounded on what was permitted
and prohibited in the courthouse. In the near future,
Blackberries and cell phones would no longer be allowed. It
was good fortune we wouldn't be there then. A family member
would be watching our children as we got through this week. It
would be imperative to stay in touch. Our courtroom was on
the eighth floor. Frequent breaks outside of the building would
be impossible. The beginning of a trial is boring – even as the
plaintiff. I sat there and Jim worked. Most of the time solo.
Defense counsel could have fielded its own softball team on a
lunch break. The jury pool was instructed briefly on the case
they may be asked to sit for. At which point the judge asked if
any potential jurors had conflicts they needed to address with
him. More than three-quarters lined up to be excused by the
judge in his chambers on special circumstances. Though only
the lawyers were permitted for this part of jury selection, Jim
kept me abreast of what was happening.

"One guy, before hearing any evidence, claimed, 'You can't hold a doctor responsible for the death of a baby.'" So that is what we were up against. Eventually the jury was selected and opening remarks began at 2 in the afternoon. As I watched the jury enter, I felt guilty but so grateful for their presence. Any one of them could have been doing something more meaningful for themselves and a loved one – yet they were here for James. Perhaps they would never know, but despite the outcome, I was grateful to their time.

Jim introduced himself to the jury and began to introduce James. How old he was. What happened for him to arrive before them in memoriam via the legal system.

There was a large flat screen hung high on the wall behind the judge. I pictured James there. He was here. Jim's opening would be full of information I already knew. I focused on my demeanor. I tried hard not to try to be anything. I could feel the eyes looking at me, sizing me up. It was my actions that were on trial.

There was a lot of technical background for the jury to understand the argument Jim would make. Focus would be on the early extubation, late re-intubation, absent providers, and arrest of October 4, 2001. He made it clear that no one would testify that James died of anything that he was born with.

The defense counsel stood up and acknowledged the severity of the case. He chose to define "attending physician" as one who is "on call." These are the sort of subtleties of the English language where the medical community uses the language that should be more readily defined to its patients. Given the understanding that I could not be with my son because the doctors would be watching him closely was misleading. In part, it led to this mutually uncomfortable experience for plaintiff and defendant. Had I known the doctor was "on call" I would have demanded to remain alongside my postoperative newborn baby boy. These doctors take this very seriously. Their experience and qualification were being questioned. It was not my place to question that. However, my son's life and future were gone.

Jim called me as the first witness. Dressed in the same yellow dress I wore to his funeral I moved past the eyes of the twelve jurors and two alternates. It was a summer dress with a rosebud pattern. I had trouble finding shoes to match. I ended up in a small-heeled, cream-colored slide. I was absolutely not comfortable. It was what I had. It did create closeness to James, which supported a strength and conviction. Having shared countless hours of discussions with Jim in person, by phone, through email and even written letters, I did feel safe as he asked me questions. Nevertheless, I was nervous and worried.

After laying the groundwork of the pregnancy and early interactions with doctors and tests, the discussions focused on Jim's argument.

"After you saw him in the four o'clock time period, did anybody tell you they were going to pull the tube out?"

"Yes. I was told they were getting ready to take him off the ventilator. I asked them, is that not too soon? Is he going to be okay? They said that…"

Defense spoke up, "Objection, Your Honor."

Jim quickly fixed it, "Do you recall who it was that said that."

I identified the nurse by name. Then I went through the evening's events as I experienced them. I remained guarded for the bulk of direct examination. However, I lost composure when I talked about holding James after he died.

"Subsequent to you going through all this, did you ever get an understanding as to why this parade of horrible occurred?"

I sure had not - not before starting the legal process. I understand now.

My cross-examination would wait for the next day. It was a fraction in length compared to my deposition. Perhaps the tears encouraged the defense to wrap it up quickly. The defense counsel began to question my decision on the lack of an autopsy. The idea of my baby being cut open and explored more brought tortuous tears from my eyes.

"Yesterday, I heard your testimony, Mrs. Mannix, that the point where you were asked whether or not you wanted an autopsy performed that your feeling at that time was that he had been handled enough. You did not want that happen is that correct?"

"That's correct."

"I appreciate that. But my question is; do you think this autopsy – did you have an understanding that the autopsy may have been able to tell you about something that happened to James?"

I could feel the lump in my throat growing. I felt like an idiot. Perhaps an autopsy would have saved us all the trouble of four years of legal wrangling and a week in the courtroom. "My understanding was these doctors had seen my son inside and out, that someone there would be able to explain to me and tell me what happened." The dam of tears was about to burst, "I did not think an autopsy would tell us anything more at that point. I didn't think there was ever going to be a reason [for James's death] that someone wouldn't be able to tell me."

"You didn't think at that time that an autopsy would give you some additional information about what happened to James?"

Full tears were flowing, make up running, "No, I did not."

With that he excused me like a used napkin at a drive-thru. I was more a defendant than the doctors. There was something I had done wrong. Simply suing a doctor is wrong anymore. Forget what may have led to the decision. It was a foregone conclusion that unless I walk away with millions of dollars, I was wrong to take legal action. Yet, especially, if I walked away with cash, I was not only wrong but also a "money-grubbing slime" trying to make a buck off her son's death. Whatever I wore, however I held myself, whatever I said was first evidence to my intention in litigation.

The judge looked to Jim as I sat there clinging to my full tissues, "any redirect?"

"No, sir." Thank God for Jim. Even if he had a redirect, he was letting me off the stand. The pain was enormous. Trying to remain composed, I was shaking from the inside. I could see James dead in the hospital isolette, purple, black, and blue. By not authorizing an autopsy, it was somehow my fault that he was in that condition at all. I knew I should thank these people who had taken off work, and are away from their families so I could tend to mine. I wanted to speak directly to them but was ashamed for my role in bringing them there. I carefully looked toward a couple of them. Some of the jurors were crying with me.

The judge directed, "You may step down."

With all the respect he could muster, Jim coldly directed without preface, "Dr. Kochilas."

Sadly, I watched this doctor be questioned in court. I had hoped to maintain a respective, appreciative relationship with the caregivers who cared for James. This adversarial relationship was as unexpected for me as they would say the "event" was for them. During his courtroom testimony and in the years following trial, I would search for how we went from partners in care to opposing plaintiff and defendant. It was telling that he distanced himself from the Nemours Cardiac Center in the year following James's death. There was hope in that. Jim and Michael, however, didn't hold out that hope.

Dr. Kochilas' testimony in court was more trying than in deposition. Jim and the doctor struggled it seemed to be on the same page. Dr. Kochilas was trying to repeat what his deposition testimony was. However, the difficulty he had in answering was not the same as in deposition. Though he had gone with defense counsel the day before to time his travel from the takeout place back to the hospital, he could not recall the name of the restaurant.

These are highly skilled professionals who have been required to memorize minutiae to competently perform their job. Yet, here in court, remembering anything was a struggle.

"I was not there so I cannot comment on that"

"I do not understand your question."
"I do not know."

These were the themes of all the answers.

Hand-off is a particularly threatening time for patients. If the doctor caring for you now was not there earlier, cannot speak to the condition or care earlier, it leaves the patient in harm's way since the continuity of care is implausible. Certainly there was a better way to take care of the doctor's needs taking care of the baby's needs.

Q: "Do you remember in your deposition when I asked you about what James was connected to, what monitors he had and all that; do you remember those questions?"

A: "Yes."

Q: "You told me. Tell me if I am wrong. There was this telemetry type thing where he has continuous monitoring of his respiratory rate, his heart rate, all that stuff on the screen?

A: "Yes."

Q: "Is it not a fact that you told me that after this happened, you went back and actually looked at and printed out that data that was in that equipment and looked at it.

A: "I don't know if I printed, but I found the printed report, correct."

Jim confirmed, "You found the printed report?"

A: "I saw a printed report."

Q: "Of tracings?"

"Yes," Dr. Kochilas confirmed.

Q: "You saw that?"

A: "Yes."

Q: "Those tracings would provide us very important information, would they not, about second to second minute by minute, hour to hour breathing rate, heart rate, blood pressure, everything?"

Dr. Kochilas answered with an honesty that was hard to find from the other defendants and defense expert, "I believe so."

Q: "It is not here is it, sir?"

A: "I did not see that when I looked through the chart, when it was given to me for review, I did not see that."

Q: "You saw that when you were in the hospital though didn't you sir?"

A: "I saw that. Yes."

The courtroom had grown quite silent as this exchange progressed. No one was even distracted enough to fidget.

"Isn't that," Jim continued, "we are looking now at a flow sheet that has hour-by-hour recordings or maybe 15 minutes by 15 minutes. That document, that piece of information that would give us the second-by-second information about James Mannix, we could really follow what happened, it is gone; is that right, sir?"

"Yes, I don't have that."

"Don't have that. Do you know where it is?"

"I don't know," Dr. Kochilas replied.

Nearly two years after verdict, I sat down with this doctor, one on one, face to face. He was surprised to learn that the first request for medical records had come personally from me. Not a legal representative. He explained that the practice in the hospital is/was as soon as someone asks for records the hospital lawyers are informed, they look at the records first, and the doctors involved are warned.

As soon as Jim was finished with his questioning, defense counsel stepped up. "Do you treat your patients based on a computer print out, what a computer says is normal?"

"No."

"Mr. Beasley asked you whether you had made any notations on the flow sheet about James's condition; is that something you would normally do?"

"No."

"You did write a note in this case, didn't you following?"

"I did. If there is something important to comment on, then I have to write a note," Dr. Kochilas commented.

"But not on the flow sheet?"

"Not on the flow sheet."

Defense counsel established it would not be the doctor's responsibility to maintain records for the patient.

Jim began his redirect with an apology for any misspeaking regarding whether he wrote a note on the flow sheet or elsewhere. There was some clarity gained in that the doctor did not make it a practice to write a note at the onset of his care of his patient if there were no concerns.

"Is it your position, sir, when a new doctor comes on duty they don't have to write a note saying I have come in and seen the patient, he is stable. He is not. Is it your position when you come on duty you don't have to do anything except to go get take-out?"

"This is correct," Dr. Kochilas replied, "not a usual practice to write a note if there is nothing in particularly that you need to comment on." Perhaps, continuous monitoring of patients could be improved with the use of technology.

"You were asked about these tracings and what your understanding of hospital policy was. Is it not a fact that these tracings that are not in the chart, not available to this jury, to see the second to second, minute by minute fluctuations of this baby's life are gone, are they important information for the medical chart?"

"It is part of the information. I would love to have them," Dr. Kochilas said.

Jim acknowledged Dr. Kochilas' responsibility as James's physician and not a risk manager for the hospital. "As far as information so these folks in the jury can figure out why this child died, those tracings would contain more information than any other piece of information in this chart, more than the flow sheet, more than the progress notes, more than anything, is that right?"

"Correct."

"It is missing from the chart, is it not?"

"It is missing," Dr. Kochilas further confirmed.

My heart was broken all over again as the physician dressed in an expensive green suit moved away from the witness stand with his head hanging low, walked past me and returned to his seat next to his co-defendant. I would love to have had the tracings too. We both may have been a pawn in someone else's chess game. It is hard to validate the purpose of the rest of the trial save to learn that the judge was defense's best-kept secret.

The judge compared my attorney to the bumbling – television investigator, Columbo. This proved to only show the judge's age but also Jim's quick wit. Like it or not, Jim may have been born to a legendary legal eagle but his intelligence was all his own. Jim did not become an MD to make for an easier career. He became a doctor because that is what he wanted to do. Life has greater plans for most of us if we give it the chance to show us. As Jim prepared for a career in Genetics, he started a family and priorities began to shift. Bred to make the most of his capabilities and advantages, Jim worked to receive a law degree after already having a medical degree and a young family. Family and healing. Jim was able to be present for his family while helping someone heal. Despite the tumultuous times for both our families, his professional skills were helping someone else heal. That is what brought him in front of a judge who didn't know how to meet wits with him.

I went home those evenings of the first week of October 2005, envisioning the judge's delayed reaction to a "Jim-ism" earlier in court. The judge would drive home, sit down for a meal with his wife and in the middle of a report on daily activities he might laugh out loud or share that "A-ha" moment. It was then, he understood Jim's carefully worded, sparsely shared commentary of a courtroom event. The judge waffled in his treatment of the offense. At times he worked painstakingly hard and long to explain why he would not rule in our favor. Other times, from the layperson's view, he worked hard to not be just. The judge never interrupted defense in front of the jury. Jim's legal flow was interrupted at least four times by the Judge with the jury in attendance.

Michael and I went home that week of trial and struggled as we had the four previous years. We still lived in the same house, raised our children as two, but we did not sleep in the same place nor share the depths of our sadness. Perhaps we were blaming each other. We also may have just been denying ourselves any joy. Michael wanted us to hold hands in front of the jury. I would not have it. Even if counsel wouldn't ask us how much the loss had hurt our marriage, I wouldn't lie in action. This death affected every area of our lives.

During the trial, Dr. Raphaely was forced to return to these issues of blood gas values, ventilation, and oxygenation. Jim asked, "Let me understand something. When you saw them, Mr. and Mrs. Mannix, in the intensive care unit after the event, did you tell them that there was a malfunction of the ventilator?"

"I don't believe I did, no." Raphaley said.

After having defended his position with his own counsel that he would have been forthcoming with any information available to him to help me as a parent understand what had happened with my son, Raphaely was being asked to further demonstrate the validity of his statements.

"You have the original note there. Would you be kind enough to find the note that you wrote in the chart that says, hey, we had a problem with the ventilator, we did this, we did that, and everything is fine now?"

"No, there is no note in there."

"Nobody, not just you, but nobody mentions anywhere in that chart that there was a broken ventilator that was breathing this child early on; is that right?" Jim asked.

"No, there isn't. Nevertheless, it did occur."

There was a lot *not* in the record.

This was a horrifying admission. Not just the admission but more so that this physician of thirty years was using this as a defense for the care provided. Where was the oversight? Who oversees the products used in accredited hospitals to ensure safety in their utilization by physicians for medical treatment? Was it to be inferred that since there was a broken ventilator, he the anesthesiologist/intensivist and co-director was not responsible?

James's presence in the courtroom was there and palpable. He was there in the silence of the jury, in the panicked whispers of the excess defense counselors, in the audible gasp of a court reporter and in the focus of plaintiffs' counsel.

"Isn't the medical chart supposed to contain information that's pertinent to the care and treatment received by the patient?"

"Yes. Doesn't include everything however."

Jim delved farther, "Well, the pertinent things -- I guess one pertinent thing, can't we agree, when a child is just out of deep hypothermic circulatory arrest and cardiopulmonary bypass and breathing through a ventilator, the ventilator is broken and it's giving bad blood gases, you don't think that's something important that should be in the chart?"

"It may be. But it's not in the record and it did occur," Raphaely stated clearly.

"Is Nemours Cardiac Center accredited by the Joint Council of Accreditation of Hospitals?"

"Within the hospital for children, yes."

"So you're accredited by JCAHO, in other words?"

"As part of the hospital, yes." Tension was building in the courtroom as the doctor attempted to become more evasive with his answers. He re-adjusted his position on the witness stand several times. He fidgeted with his glasses. The arrogance that he had presented in deposition and to the jury was becoming a challenge to maintain. Raphaely didn't know where Jim's questioning, specifically, was headed.

" What does the JCAHO say about maintaining medical records?"

"What I said," Raphaely tersely replied.

But what did he say? He didn't say anything regarding JCAHO's requirements for records maintenance. His answer was very vague.

Jim didn't stop. "And it's a fact, sir, is it not, that in the time period that James is being treated, not just paper portions of the chart were to be maintained in its entirety, but also all the computer data, is that also correct?"

"No, that isn't true."

"That's not right?"

"No," Raphaely testified under oath.

Jim had to ask, "Have you ever read the JCAHO hospital accreditation standards that deal with medical records and the retaining -- the retention of both paper and computer data for medical records?"

Adjusting again, the doctor replied, weakly, "I don't know whether I read that specific section."

"Would you like me to read it to you?"

"Go ahead."

Jim read to the class of varying backgrounds with particular focus to the board-certified, seasoned medical professional: "The hospital develops and implements measures to safeguard data information, including the clinical record against loss, destruction, and tampering. That includes among other things retrieving baseline data if original records are lost, destroyed, or tampered with. For computerized systems, the hospital has a process for disaster recovery and business continuity that would impact the management information."

"Now you heard Dr. Kochilas testify about the data that came out of the telemetry information; correct, sir?"

"I did hear that, yes," Raphaley said looked to his defense. It seemed he was hoping for an objection or some well-timed interruption. It didn't arrive just yet.

" Where is that information so that the folks of the jury can view the second-by-second, minute-by-minute, hour-by-hour data that came from the monitoring of James, not just the flow sheet?"

And then, as plaintiff was making a valid and frightening point, it was even too much for the judge to accept. He offered pause in Jim's momentum.

The judge asked, "May I see the book please?"

"Yes, sir," he complied approaching the bench with the JCAHO guidelines in hand.

Despite the expert medical providers acknowledging the importance of this mysteriously missing piece to James's medical record, the Judge could not understand any reason for a spoliation charge to the jury. "Spoliation" is the legal term of "the willful destruction of evidence or the failure to preserve potential evidence for another's use in pending or future litigation." It is appropriate for sanctions to be administered by a judge for the spoliation of evidence, "whether negligent or intentional, even where the loss of potential evidence occurs before an action has been commenced, if a litigant or its expert knows or reasonably should know that the evidence might be relevant to a possible action" (Vecchione 2003). Whether negligent or intentional this was a loss of evidence that was relevant to the explanation of what happened to James.

Medical records can be tampered and manipulated to the point that they are not safe in the hands of trusted medical professionals. The possibility that from within the halls of the places in America held dear by all as a safe haven for the sick and a place of miracle delivery, these same places, hospitals, could actually harbor individuals who would breach such trust. That a gray haired, eloquent physician would actually not know what the accreditation requirements were for his work was cause for pause.

" I will apply dietetic measures for the benefit of the sick according to my ability and judgment; I will keep them from harm and injustice."

"To hold him who has taught me this art as equal to my parents and to live my life in partnership with him, and if he is in need of money to give him a share of mine."

Portions of The Hippocratic Oath

Trial was a clear fork in the road of this mom's life. The divergent paths were marked "Law School" and "Health Care." I would need to take time to understand which direction would be most effective. While the lawsuit was pending it would be best to just sit at the crossroads marked Plaintiff's side of a courtroom. As I sat in my seat, watched and listened to the ongoing testimony, a force began to push without apology down one path over the other.

The nurse practitioner had told my sister the night after James's event, "we lost him." It was my sister who was the first to tell me. I physically collapsed onto the linoleum floor of the hallway of unit 2B. While I lay there I wondered, why I had to hear this from my sister. The HIPAA laws had been enacted. This was the first time my sister had even been to the hospital. I was reminded of that transgression as nurse practitioner, Barbara, gave her trial testimony but couldn't seem to figure out what her own answers should be. The long, arduous pauses of the nurse Ray, in deposition were comparable to the long pauses being taken in court by this nurse practitioner.

She had just managed her direct examination by her counsel. With impeccable experience and references, I was amazed that she was here. It didn't seem to fit that she wouldn't be competent to run a code let alone answer technical questions of her specialized trade of fifteen plus years. Her testimony as defense was as you would expect mine would be as plaintiff. The interest is always in the cross.

Jim approached collegially with his questions. "You were on a 24 – hour shift?"

"Yes, sir."

That is an excessively long workday. However, some consider it less risky than having too many hand-offs where important, relevant patient information can be lost or forgotten. Sign offs can be like a game of 'Whisper down the Lane'. The success of the game is dependent on the concentration of the individual for the whole.

"You weren't at the bedside when this event occurred, were you?"

"Not standing at the bedside, no."

"You weren't in the unit were you?"

"I'm not positive I don't recall." Yet, I recalled from her deposition a different answer. It had been mentioned she had gone to the cafeteria for dinner. I wanted to encourage her, tell her, it's okay. Just tell the truth. Understandably, anyone on a shift watching two sunrises will need to eat.

Jim continued, "In caring for James, did you develop an understanding that his respiratory rate was going up and up and up and his oxygen saturations were going down as a trend?"

"I'd have to look at the flow sheet." Fair response.

"Did you look at the flow sheet before testifying today?"

"Yes. Thank you."

"Could you just tell us what the readings on the chart are between four and six o'clock for his respiratory rate?" Jim asked.

"Sure. 44, 60, and 80." Here we go. I looked over at the jury. One juror who wore an Eagles' jersey seemed disinterested. He was getting sleepy. It was a struggle to maintain attention for the science of my son's death.

"And 80 is too high isn't it?"

Barbara replied having well established her expertise earlier, "80 is high."

"You felt that he was breathing at that rate because he was really trying to get rid of carbon dioxide; isn't that right?"

"I'm not sure how to answer that question."

"When I asked you at your deposition, you didn't have trouble. You told me it was because he was trying to blow off the CO2."

She concurred, "People do increase their respiratory rate to blow off a high CO2, yeah." I imagined that looks like someone gasping for air.

The medically trained lawyer and the advanced practice nurse continued back and forth discussing physiology far beyond most bachelor's degrees. Despite the unfamiliar terms, the jury and courtroom could see the tensions rising again between defense witness and plaintiff's counsel. Their tension was engaging. We were finally getting somewhere.

Jim summed up the discussion, "In fact, the high CO_2 resulted in something that I think you previously referred to as a compensative respiratory acidosis, is that right?"

"That's what I said in my deposition," she looked to defense counsel and the defendants. She was nervous and insecure. It was uncomfortable to watch. It got worse.

"Do you stand by that today?"

She didn't answer. The nurse practitioner fumbled her gaze between the flow sheet in front of her and the defense table to her right. The jury sat and stared. Jim didn't move. She didn't receive any help from defense counsel.

Respiratory acidosis occurs when the lungs are not exchanging its gases adequately which causes a buildup of carbon dioxide in the lungs. Carbon dioxide is an acid. A healthy competent physiology answers this imbalance through engaging a metabolic process. James's kidneys got rid of the excess acid. Even though his gases were still not adequately exchanging in his lungs, James was able to rectify his situation through all his healthy organs. In doing so he managed a compensated respiratory acidosis. James, at two days of age and hours post unnecessary open heart surgery, had effectively given a chance for his healthcare providers to fix the ventilation problem. Fix the broken medical equipment that was supposedly JCAHO accredited. Fix the lowered standard of care by allowing him more time to rest his lungs and get the breathing tube back down his throat. He had only two days of breathing outside of me. James just wasn't so sick. The pinched aorta was all that needed a little widening. Every organ and system in him was perfect and beautiful. No one was around to take the opportunity James had given them.

At long last the nurse practitioner answered with a question, "Looking at which blood gas?"

"It was your words, not mine, ma'am." Gloves were off. Jim had had it too. He was throwing everything in the ring. The nurse was running away from the baby that lay dead in a cemetery an hour away. Integrity had arrived in the courtroom as a personal injury attorney. Not a nurse. Maybe the nurse was afraid of losing a job.

"I understand that." The nurse went on as she looked through the chart.

"Trying to see if you stand by that."

"The 7.46, 57, 201 plus 13 with a bicarb of 37 looks like a compensated metabolic alkalosis.

"Are you talking about before he was extubated, all right, that was his blood gas?"

"Yes."

"That was the 16:00 blood gas one minute before he was extubated. Now, when your deposition was taken, we were talking about the post extubation, the post removing of the breathing tube blood gases. Am I wrong when I read your deposition and I listened to your words that you said it was actually a compensated respiratory acidosis?" Jim was looking for clarification.

"No, you're not wrong." she replied.

"Do you stand by the fact that you're saying it was a compensated respiratory acidosis today?"

He took another long pause. So extensive a pause it is documented in the trial transcripts.

"No, I don't think so."

"You don't stand by it?" Jim asked.

"No," she replied in a near whisper.

Re-cross was successful for her team in that defense allowed her to further explain these alien figures that made sense to the medically trained. He ended with the question, "Is that abnormal?"

Her response was, "No."

At which time, Jim jumped back in the ring armed with the truth and an ability to understand it. He handed and asked her to read her deposition testimony.

"Under my name?"

"Your deposition."

"Why don't you go to page 41, line 7 to line 14 to see if that refreshes your recollection." Jim walked off a few calories as the court waited for the nurse to catch up.

"Okay," she conceded.

"What was your answer to the question: Does it look to you like this is a compensated respiratory acidosis giving you the normal pH but a 13 base excess and high pCO2? Is that a compensated respiratory acidosis?'"

She read, "That's a compensated respiratory acidosis."

Jim reinforced his point by explaining to the jury, with the nurse practitioner's help, how after giving deposition an errata sheet, where the deposed can read and make any necessary changes to the testimony occurs. She read and signed it without changing her testimony. Surprisingly, defense counsel re-entered. He referred her to the following page of her testimony and had her read one line by giving latitude and longitude coordinates but not context. Nurse read, "I don't know if I recall a compensated respiratory acidosis because the pH is normal."

Jim pounced, "Wait a minute. You honor, may I?"

But, the judge had already with uncharacteristic energy, force and volume directed the bailiff, "Why don't you take the jury out!"

The jury stood while looking at their peers with rolling eyes, half-cocked grins, and shaking heads. There was a gaper delay getting out of the box as they looked at defense and plaintiff tables. I could agree with the judge completely when he informed counsel that "the jury has no idea what compensated respiratory acidosis is." They did understand that something was inherently wrong with the nurse's testimony. It would take me years to understand compensated respiratory acidosis. Then when I got it, it just clicked. It is the basic metabolic response a body gives when trying to operate without enough oxygen in the lungs. It sounds big and scary and complicated. It is not, especially for the medically trained.

After a lengthy editorial from the judge on the exchange, Jim decided to move on. I leaned over, "Jim, the jury is going to wonder why. Maybe they should get more of an explanation?" Jim would not go farther.

It was done. He was forced to cut his losses. He, like I, learned how to deal with that fact of life. There was more to the legal wrangling than I could foresee. I could see after her appearance that I would not take the nursing path. I would never want to find myself in the position that I could not say what I knew to be true. I would not be put in the position of heralding my expertise and dedication to patients but a patient's memory would be abused from worry for job security. I envied the judge. He was the one with the real power over the health care system. Yet, I despised how he was utilizing his position.

He was a stocky fellow with a somewhat carefree manner. He didn't edit much of what he verbalized from the bench. He was anxious for others to understand how much work he had without ever going into specifics. His comments made me realize he wanted to wrap up our case. He considered his other matters more important than James's. At times, my son's case was really handled like a free period for him; a high school study hall. He read over other issues from the bench, he reminisced with the defense expert, Wessel, about mutual friends and acquaintances, and asked for guidance on how quickly counsel would wrap up all the while adding, "I won't hold you to it but..." At a break in Wessel's testimony, he excused the court but said he would stay on the bench. He wanted to ask the defense expert a question, "It has nothing to do with the case."

"Sure, "Jim replied. It was like my boss asking me if she could take a coffee break. How was counsel to deny the judge?

Wessel appeared flattered and happy to oblige. Defense was as well. The lawyers, doctors, and my husband all moved along. I stayed in my place and fumbled through an empty purse. I did not appreciate this disregard for fair process. If the judge in my son's case was going to be talking to the defense witness during trial, it was my right to eavesdrop.

"So when were you at William and Mary?" he asked Wessel.

Big smiles accompanied the dates of his attendance. Further discussion ensued about their mutual alum friends, peers, and associates. This appeared to be a conflict of interest. Everything that happened in the courtroom was about the case. Certainly everything the judge did and said. But I was new at all of it. Just like the hospital. The jargon and activities were taken for granted for those that commonly frequent the place. An objective observer can identify areas for improvement.

From this discussion forward the court's decisions favored the defense ad nauseum.

The defense expert argued that everything that was done in my son's care is exactly how it would be done at his current institution. Everything was standard. Research in Jim's firm uncovered a text identified as Moss and Adams, 2001. Dr. Wessel had written a chapter. He specifically wrote, "This sensitivity to stimuli and liability in hemodynamic response may be expressed as sudden death during the first postoperative night following apparently successful and uncomplicated congenital heart surgery." Jim's argument was that a full term infant who was otherwise healthy and underwent open-heart surgery required a good twenty-four rest on a ventilator. Wessel's work argued the same. After reading the quote Jim asked Dr Wessel's opinion, "Do you agree with that?"

Without hesitation, defense expert answered, "Yes."

Defense stepped in: "Your honor, I'd ask if he can show the article to the witness so he can answer." The judge allowed the break in flow.

Jim asked the witness if he would like to see the textbook he wrote.

"Yes."

"Moss and Adams, you wrote a chapter in that?"

"I coauthored a chapter in Moss and Adams. Can you tell me what particular edition we're talking about?"

"2001. These books right here." Jim lifted two identical texts from a box at his side and showed the court. "Do you have a copy of them in your library?"

"I may not. I don't recognize the cover, but it – I know that I've written – co-authored chapters in Moss and Adams, " the witness replied with great control.

With less control the judge again interjected, "Hold on. Take the jury out."

He went on once the jury was gone, "So we can avoid objections and discussions in front of the jury, if there are a series of books or articles of which you intend to rely, let's establish a protocol so we don't wave it around because cute doesn't go over real well here. It really doesn't." Cute? Pointing out textbooks a well-paid defense expert helped co-author during the wrongful death trial of a child would not be defined as "cute."

With professionalism and humor, the lawyer stepped back in the line the judge wanted him in, "Understood. The box has more than books in it, by the way."

"Yea. I mean," the judge began," I don't have any problem with you doing it. I just wanted to stop it before it got out of hand because I could see Mr. Wessel was about to jump up and say something which I probably would find objectionable. So I just thought I'd cut it off right now. So we all understand what the ground rules are now?" The judge now had a personal relationship with the defense expert witness. There was no doubt he could anticipate his reactions with such accuracy.

"Yes, sir." Jim appeased.

Defense paid for a good expert witness. He had credentials, acceptable features, and a steady-trained demeanor on the stand. His testimony completely agreed with that of the defendants' and was strengthened with his own words of "luxuriant" and "absolutely yes" or 'positively not." Perhaps the good doctor would like to experience the "luxury" of an oxygen level of 52.

Jim went straight to the point, "In the 2001 book you say: 'all neonates after cardiopulmonary bypass get postoperative intubation through the night.' You don't list in here, except patients with coarctation, do you?"

The expert finished his answer, "There is no question in my mind that the 2001 standard of care did not dictate that patients who had repair of Hypoplastic aortic arch needed to be ventilated through the night. That is absolutely not the standard of care."

James did not have a hypoplastic aortic arch. He had a discrete coarctation of the aorta. Hypoplastic wasn't mentioned in his records or reports until after the cardiopulmonary arrest. The jury however was only getting to hear what the judge wanted them to hear. I was beginning to sense we were being bullied into submission. The tone of the fight changed.

"The work goes on, the cause endures, the hope still lives

and the dreams shall never die."

~ *Senator Edward Kennedy*

The week was coming to a close. Instead of the sun and blue sky of this week four years ago, each day was gray, rainy and cold. The atmosphere inside matched the weather outside. It was not a good week but I was okay. My worries now were for Jim. Being told to come up with a figure we could bring to Arbitration was a distasteful pill to swallow despite Jim's warnings. There is no price fair for a child, his life, his dreams, his future, the missed holidays, and the family he would never meet. There is no one that can dictate how much they would pay for my anguish over his death either. Somehow, just two weeks previous we met that challenge as well. Arbitration was a requirement of this activity. To "settle" would mean to also accept a confidentiality agreement.

Paying such a steep price was a struggle. My son was already silenced. With money, I could blanket his grave. I'd rather keep his memory alive by finding the way to save another from this tragedy. A ray of hope still flickered for physicians. Who wanted to settle, the docs or their defense counsel? A couple weeks before going to court, I walked into the small arbitration room that was suffocated by a rectangular boardroom table. I knew I needed to entertain the settlement idea. I wanted answers. Thanks to Jim and his firm I received them. I would never be able to reimburse his time, resources and expenses without a financial award. A financial award also would create a launch pad to encourage a change. This is the only way we have to discipline negligent professionals.

Jim had prepared us. We were ready. The defense counsel was already present. By the time we sat down, we were escorted back out and sat in a room across the hall. The arbitrator spoke to defense then reported back to us. They absolutely will not go to seven figures.

"Fuck 'em." Jim instructed the arbitrator. I laughed out loud then and still do every time I recall the exchange. He had taken the words right out of my mouth.

Then he looked at me, the lone lady in the room, and apologized.

"For what! I am with you completely," I said.

It was a time-consuming waste of many people's precious time. Before the meeting, papers were passed back and forth between attorneys' offices with figures on them. The numbers go up and down and ideally get closer and closer. If the defense feels plaintiff is at a dollar figure close to what they can consider, the arbitration meeting goes forward. Clearly, defense traveled several states to keep the chess game alive. Every step I took led me into the courtroom on the fourth anniversary of the very events being argued.

It had been four years since I sat next to James's bed while he was on ECMO. As both legal teams finished their closing statements and the judge prepared the jury for their deliberations, it seemed like yesterday that James was suffering. I did not want to leave the hospital. I would appreciate the awful troubles other souls struggled with that were surely worse than mine. The one-month memorial service for 9/11 in the hospital chapel was a perfect opportunity. Composure and respect was maintained. I sat at my child's bedside, asked his caretakers how *they* were doing, spoke to my older children with a smile and forced enthusiasm, managed to eat a bit each day, expressed breast milk through a machine, tended to my hygiene as if there were no troubles. God would certainly be moved to send a miracle. I was certain that God would personally touch one of these physicians to know exactly what to do and when to save his life...and deliver the miracle. Just as things were going my way, a force took over and took my son. He died on a Saturday morning with a machine as his last companion.

I never held my son alive again. Instead, I received 9 days of moments to hope, pray, caress, sing to, and love this adorable baby boy. The baby was given 9 days of moments to listen, fight, smell, heal, feel, and be loved. Everyone dies. No one knows when. Engaging the knowledge of a medically trained professional is a request for help in easing the pain, burden and uncertainty in life's last guarantee. A well-trained and counseled provider can hear to what extent the help is requested and to admit when he can do no more. Whether a few more years are the result of the doctor's hand, a few more days or just a minute, he hasn't performed a miracle. He has provided a treasured moment.

Fast forward four years and I didn't care about what God planned. I didn't believe He was even in the room. I did bargain with Him again, though; not for me and not for James, but for Jim and his family. At some point, if there was a God, perhaps He could show himself now and deliver a just verdict. The process gave structure to an undefined need. Yet, it really was all in the hands of the judge. He began:

"Ladies and gentleman, you have now heard all of the evidence that is going to be presented in this case." After reiterating the complaint my husband and I brought forth on behalf of our deceased eleven-day-old son, definitions and how to apply them to the case were given, the judge continued, "A corporation is considered a person within the meaning of the law. As an artificial person, a person, a corporation, can only act through its servants, agents or employees. If you find that any of the corporation's personnel were negligent in performing their duties at the time of the incident, then the corporation is also negligent."

Judge Toliver explained to the jury, "In a civil case like this the burden of proof is a preponderance of evidence." The jury would only see one picture of James. Yet, we were fortunate to have half dozen photos of him eating, sleeping, gazing. My favorite shows his whole face, beautiful features and intense eyes gazing directly at you. The jury would see one that shielded his face from full view.

I was stunned and expected a defense outcome of the jury's deliberations when I heard the following for the first time as read by the judge:

"The law, therefore, requires that the conduct of the defendants be judged by the degree of care, skill, and diligence exercised by health care providers if the same field and/or specialty. ... Each health care provider, which includes nurses and doctors, is held to the standard of care and knowledge commonly possessed by members of his or her profession and/or specialty in good standing. It is not the standard of care of the most highly skilled, nor is it necessarily that of average members of this profession since who have less than average skills, may still possess the degree if skill and care to treat patients competently."

The defendants in the courtroom did not intend for James to die. The system in which they were working put my son's life in grave danger. After the unpleasant experience of litigation, the same health care system has shown it put their livelihoods at great risk as well. Doctors and nurses pledge to "do no harm." When harm unfortunately occurs during the course of health care delivery, there is an effect on patient and provider. Understandably, the patient has more to lose. However, the providers should not be encouraged by the institutions they help to "prop up" by sacrificing their own moral code when a patient or patient's family ask, "What happened? Please help me understand."

The jury took a number of hours to deliberate. I thought it would have been a quicker turnaround. More waiting. For a little bit, Jim and I waited together on a bench of the eighth floor of a downtown building next to a wall sized window, looking out on a very gray cold October Friday. Having done all he could at that point, Jim seemed to relax a little bit.

"You know, I'm not the only Jim Beasley, Jr."

With an uncertain laugh, I replied "Uh, ok. You're the only one for me."

"Down in Florida we just placed a grave stone marked 'James E Beasley, Jr.' on the grave of my brother. My dad's first baby boy was stillborn."

Huh. The old guy really did get it.

Jim went on to share how his father's life was shaped and re-worked after the stillbirth of his oldest son and Jim's only brother. Jim mentioned the tattoo he wore now on his upper arm which reads "Tommy". I wondered how much Jim ever shared of Tommy. At times over the years I worried that I was putting too much on Jim. Worried a bit for myself too. There were no family and friends waiting out the deliberation with us. He was my support system through this whole process. Regardless of the outcome, I was staring down another loss. Of all the words both written and spoken that we had shared, this conversation was a gift. I can't speak for him, but the remainder of that day, I considered the silent force these very small, quickly lost young lives actually are. So many of them had been lost. A deeper grief would be loose once freed of the legal muzzle.

This gray Friday afternoon preceding a three-day weekend was coming to a close. The jury returned with a verdict shortly before 5 PM. Jim slipped back into his attorney role summoning Michael and I back to the courtroom. When we were assembled in the courtroom, Jim leaned in to Michael and I with a final, experienced directive, "Whatever it is, Guys, say nothing. Do nothing. No reaction okay?"

"Sure Jim," I said. Michael nodded in compliance.

The jury filed to their seats straining to keep their eyes away from our table or that of the defense. Toliver asked a few questions. I visualized James on the large flat-screen television that rested above the bench. I pulled his socks out of my purse. I wanted him there.

The foreman answered the several questions of their deliberations. Kochilas had been found not negligent. Raphaely was found negligent. For reasons that still can only be imagined, the jury determined Raphaely's negligence to not be responsible for James's death. Nemours was determined to be not negligent, as well. Jim's passionate side revealed itself, "What?!? That makes no sense!" he shouted as he slammed his hand on the table. I looked at him. Jim repeated himself but in a hush, "That just makes no sense."

The trial ended. Jim began gathering up his papers and his briefcase. I asked the obvious, "What does that mean?"

"They get away with it, Mary Ellen. They got away with it." Jim wouldn't meet my gaze.

We walked out of the courthouse with Jim and his Delaware-counterpart. They were speaking of mistrial motions, spoliation, and appeals. I was looking for a moment to say thank you. Jim kept walking next to and talking with his peer. I was the client again. He was the attorney. This battle would be longer than imagined. Jim knew there was more he could do and he was ready for the marathon. I was disappointed in another system but I knew how to live in that condition. I was surprisingly okay. Most likely because no matter what the other parties did and didn't do, Jim had worked this case with me. I knew what to expect. I knew it was an uphill battle. I knew it didn't matter how negligent they may have been. The odds were in their favor. Finally, we stopped at the entrance to the garage. I reached out and managed an awkward embrace, "Thanks Jim. You were wonderful. I better still get a Christmas card!"

He looked toward the ground and away, "At least, they found negligence." I was mystified because he looked mortified. His work had kept me going, kept me alive. He had fought so hard. It was not an easy sight – your hero feeling ashamed.

There is an instinct in us for newness for renewal,
for a liberation of creative power.
We seek to awaken in ourselves
a force that really changes our life from within.
And yet this same instinct tell us
That this change is a recovery of that which is deepest,
most original, most personal in ourselves.

–Thomas Merton

April, 2006

I was exhausted arriving home mid-afternoon from one job knowing I would be turning around in less than an hour to the next. Yet the sky was that brilliant blue and the sun was warm. I looked forward to spending a few moments with my own children before heading out to take care of someone else's. The note on the kitchen counter from Michael said whomever had been home was now with him and off to the park. The older ones were out with friends. I took a glass of iced tea out to the porch as the mailman came up the walk.

"Hey how are you?" I asked.

"The best time of year to have my job."

"Can't think of a better place to be today – outside," I agreed.

"Yea, where's the ball player? The mailman referred to our one year old who was already talented with a ball and a bat.

"Out playing ball of course!"

"Well, at least you get a few minutes to yourself. You always have kids around you."

"Sure enough," I shout as I think about the sign hanging over the side door: "There's an Angel among us."

Placing my glass on one side and sales circulars on the other, I sat on the front step to read mail. The green and white envelope was easy to spot. My heart skipped; it was the Firm. Trial had ended six months previous but James was still bound to a Docket, a case number. Through the courts, I tried to regain the rights to my son. In life, the hospital made the decisions. Had I been the decision maker for his memory? How would he be remembered? I had forgotten that it might be coming. Jim had said that he would let us know when the decision came down on the post-trial motion. The world of civil law was slow. I wasn't expecting this so soon.

Unfortunately for James, there would be no spoliation charge to the jury for the missing records. There would be no consideration of pecuniary benefit testimony from the actuary. After the judge explained that he could find no proof for what James would have saved and earned, and as such, he would not include the actuary's testimony, it was clear what most would think. The jury would assume that a deal had been reached. The dad of a stillborn baby argues well against the majority as he stated, "Your Honor, that's the box the plaintiff is in, especially when you deal with an infant. At least if you are in an adult situation and you can look at tax returns, you can look at their behavior. It seems to be placing infants and those not yet had an opportunity to prove themselves in a different position in society."

Jim hadn't mentioned the actual date for this post-trial motion. Between scheduling, grieving his own losses, and just not needing my angst, he handled this solo. It was a surprise, but as I read, I understood. With a deep breath I cleared my mind of everything I had done already that day or would still need to do. I carefully peeled back the seal and pulled the legal size stapled papers out of the envelope. It was thicker than just a note, thinner than a day's trial transcripts. There was nothing now but the sun, the sky, this little piece of James, and I.

Listed on the first page were all the participants present that eleventh April morning in Delaware 2006. I pictured the same courtroom, saw much the same players, and heard the argument as if I was there starting with the same droll and nauseating pleasantries. All the while a baby lying in a grave. I would have to find a way to shake this reality. I kept reading. As plaintiff the responsibility to prove negligence never left even in the mistrial motion. Jim spoke with a brief overview of the inherently inconsistent jury verdict - negligent yet not responsible.

Raphaely was negligent for extubating James too early. Dr. Kochilas was found not negligent for not putting the breathing tube back in as the subsequent physician. The hospital was also jury-deemed not negligent. No one was held responsible for James's passing. Somehow the jury was able to view it as a natural event?

Jim explained, "It's inconsistent, respectfully to the jury, that there is a finding that it's negligent to pull the tube out, not negligent to put it back in, but no harm, no foul, because it didn't cause anything when the testimony was clear from almost all sides that when the breathing tube was pulled out, the oxygen levels dropped, the carbon dioxide levels increased, all of the issues that show a deteriorating health status on this newborn occurred, and, sure enough the child went into respiratory failure as a result of this tube being pulled out, and ultimate cardiac issues as well. The verdict is so inconsistent that either the jury didn't get it, or, for whatever reason, as part of the medical malpractice climate, they wanted to, no pun intended, split the baby."

I allowed myself to feel rather stupid for a long time. As a plaintiff in a wrongful death lawsuit, the experience was one of shame. People always asked what happened that my son had died. The reality that babies die from medically-induced trauma created a gaping disconnect. In living past my son, I had to stand up for him. Just because he lived a short time did not mean that he wasn't worth protecting while he was here. Infants are economically expendable in the current medico-legal climate. Yet a lot of money passed hands for my son's treatments and in withholding the truth. Living within a leading industrialized nation, its unpleasant to hear that new life can end just as quickly here as in any under-developed nation. There is an economy surrounding these babies. All I could do was shake my head. They split him.

"The concern we had with respect to your Honor's decision and charge on the economic loss issue should have gone to the jury. The box that anyone who's representing a minor or someone who hasn't worked puts these folks in a separate class than someone who has a wage loss history or has an economic history so that people can determine what was saved. I think it would be disingenuous of me to have an expert come forward and say, 'Well, even though this child only lived to ten days of life, tell us what he would have saved.'

I mean, that's impossible. You could do that with someone who's had a job. You could look at their income, the taxes, and how much they kept in the back but this entire class of people I think is a fact for the jury. It seems to be placing infants and those not yet had an opportunity to prove themselves in a different position in society," Jim shared.

The judge just didn't get this, or, chose to use his influence to move forward his personal beliefs. According to this court it would never be a matter for the jury to address unless there is proof of what an individual ten day old would have made without basing the calculations on any relative or similar circumstance. The only financial circumstance to be considered would be the evidence of what the infant earned.

Defense counsel continued to argue that James had indeed had a respiratory event but the cardiac event that occurred simultaneously was unpredictable and the true cause of death. That an intelligent human, himself a parent, can successfully argue in a modern day high court that being denied oxygen to breathe would not cause a cardiac arrest is terrifying. I do not have a medical degree. Without effective breathing, the heart will stop. This reminded me of the arguments against the abolition of slavery and women's rights to vote. This infant was simply not afforded the rights of any other "person."

Jim did his part: "Your Honor, nobody's saying that Nemours had to maintain a stack of paper. This is computer information that was gone. And whether Dr. Raphaely says to your Honor in this court something inconsistent with the standard to which this hospital is held is simply a fact issue. To the extent the Joint Commission says you keep all computer and data information, and they are audited by JCAHO, and to comply with it, they have to. This is the most important information there. It's the minute-by-minute materials. It certainly is a fact issue of circumstantial evidence why it's not there."

The judge interrupted, "Is there any evidence of fault or wrongdoing in connection with the failure to maintain that information?"

The judge had just answered his own question – it was a failure. People and institutions are to be held responsible for what they fail in. Jim had to argue through the law and not simply common decency, "Yea. There was a significant amount of circumstantial evidence. Nobody testified: 'You're right. I did it.' Nobody did that and nobody would do it. Just like Herbert vs. Lando, just because somebody denies something doesn't make it so."

Yet, in this court, the judge responded, "Now, there has to be some indication that when I didn't keep those records, I had a duty, and then I negligently failed to do that or intentionally failed to do that. Here just nobody knew what happened to them or why. They just didn't have them." This was the world in the judge's head. It seemed a distant reality that we would ever reach his thinking. After forty minutes of back and forth banter, Jim could present no more that would have any effect on the agenda this judge had thus far maintained.

The judge acknowledged freely his own juxtapositions: "Mr. Beasley, either I'm real right or I'm real wrong. And, unfortunately, from my perspective, I've been real right and I've been real wrong on numerous occasions, so I don't think any different from any other trial judge. And you have to call them as you see them and that is what the appellate court is for. And I say that with no sense of negativity or no sense of anything other than you try it, you decide, you make the rulings. I'm sure you'll take it up given the stakes. And if the Supreme Court agrees with you then we'll try it again according to what they say. I would encourage you, obviously, I don't have to, because you'll do it anyway, but to take it up. Given my place in the organization, you can get a more appropriate and better view of the case. But I'd agree it was well tried, and I think you presented an excellent case."

This judge had no idea what it was like to be a grieving parent or a plaintiff. Instead of having courage to review conflicting opinions different than his own he took the easy way out. He was so certain that someone above him would be given the opportunity to make what was wrong, or at least unclear to him, right. The judge forgot that the little boy's memory was on *his* bench. Jim's dad, who opened the door to court for me, once said. "It is true; the heart of the law is conflict." This judge passed the conflict like it was a game of Hot Potato.

This was my son's memory. I had had enough of the pain of disregard for the humanity present in our case. My son had been denied his humanity and placed in a box called fiscal irrelevance. The judge, the defense, the doctors, even the jury were wrong. The whole picture never seemed relevant to those making decisions.

The sky was still blue. My shoulders were red from sun and I was late for work. I knew the judge was real wrong. I didn't need a Supreme Court to tell me that. Given the stakes, this case - worthy or not - would not go any farther.

James was still dead.

Tommy was gone too.

Jim was willing to keep going.

Michael would oblige my decision.

I was tired.

I looked back on the agreement signed so many years ago. A simple, professional contract not binding the firm to file any motions beyond verdict. It already had. They had already done a lot with me. Broken and battered, I couldn't fight in court anymore. Jim offered encouragement and information. I needed to start picking up the pieces of James as much as Jim needed to pick up Tommy's.

Both are buried in all but our memories. This court sought to confine them there.

"Now the doctor, by virtue of accepting
science so totally,

creates a total imbalance, forgetting the art
of healing, forgetting the art of engagement,
forgetting the art of listening, forgetting the art of
caring and ceasing to invest time with the patient.
So I believe medicine has lost its human face."

~ Dr. Bernard Lown

March, 2009

"Hello. May I please speak with Dr. William Norwood?"

"This is he."

Oh, shit. I got him. Standing up to relieve sudden anxiety, I checked that my youngest was still napping.

"Dr," I choked on the title, "Norwood, this is Mary Ellen Mannix," I waited for the click.

No click. I continued, "You were involved in the care of my son at DuPont in October of 2001."

"I cared for many patients in that timeframe."

My insides were leaping through my throat. It was like saddling the horses of Chincoteague when I restrained my response to, "well, my son was James. He was born with a discrete coarctation of the aorta and he died."

"Oh yes, I think I remember him."

Jesus Christ. He thinks. It would have been better if I had thought this conversation out before I had called. However, I wasn't expecting much. My phone call to Raphaely and email to defense counsel resulted in a combined response from the latter:

"Thank you for the opportunity to discuss the case for the book you are writing. Respectfully, I write to decline that opportunity. Also, I understand you have contacted one of our clients, Dr. Raphaely. Please be advised that Dr. Raphaely does not wish to discuss the case either, and I would appreciate it if you would not contact him further about it."

Did he **appreciate** what the preventable errors my son died from gave him?

I was too anxious to get the book done and be able to say I gave Norwood the opportunity for input. So, pulling back hard on invisible reins I offered a further trigger, "I filed a lawsuit to find out what had happened to my ..."

Norwood burst in interruption, "You did not file a lawsuit to find out what happened! You filed a lawsuit for money!"

As he was coming through the phone, I was making my way through the dining room and into our kitchen. I did not want him to disturb James's little brother.

Standing in our rented kitchen, I borrowed that same Catholic school girl etiquette, but with purpose this time. It was clear this conversation, if I was to maintain composure would result in a Wii Fit-like effect on me physically. "If I had filed a lawsuit for money, then one would have expected me to take the three quarters of a million dollars offered days before trial. A gag order would have been irrelevant against the unemployed husband and lost home."

"Yes," he was a bit quieter.

"I did not take the money."

"Why?." he puzzled.

"Because I wanted to know what happened to my son; I also wanted to be able to speak freely of him."

"You should have just asked me," he replied. He went on speaking but I was stuck. I *had* asked him. Several times. His answers never changed. He didn't know what happened to my son while he was under his care. He didn't know what happened to James a month later. He did not reach out and share information without the invocation of legal proceedings.

"So, how can I help you?" He seemed annoyingly confident.

"Well, I am writing a book as part of my master's degree. It strives to reveal the healthcare and legal systems through my son's experiences in each. I am giving the opportunity to those involved in his care and his lawsuit to offer any additional thoughts or clarifications." I did not share with him how this was a testing of my own thesis. If Restorative Practices had relevance in medico-legal issues, I would have to see if they could at least work with me. I reached out to Norwood and the others to work with them in the culmination of our shared experiences. In our case, all legal timelines had been exhausted. Could I speak to someone I believed was responsible for my son's death without it being a betrayal of his memory? Would I return to homicidal fantasies? Even if not clearly stated, this would act as an opportunity for accountability to be taken by Norwood. It wasn't necessary for extensive preparation for the call. The past seven years were prep work for this moment. From that first meeting with Jim, and receiving unexpected, welcome support, to the first deposition that left me nauseous for the superficiality of pleasantries, to the regular conversations with Dr. Nick about the challenges quality surgeons face, it was all connected now. A community had been built in which I felt safe to ask what I wanted to know and whom had the answer.

"I don't have his records in front of me but I will try to answer what I can," he said. I would have to make clear to him that there was very little that I wanted from him in terms of clinical explanations. Jim had gotten those.

"I actually know a good deal of what happened. At least, all that I will ever be allowed to know." That grabbed him.

"Allowed? What do you mean allowed?"

I took another deep breath and steadied myself in one place instead of wearing tracks in the linoleum. "Yes. Allowed. There remains missing a key piece of James's medical records."

He seemed dismayed by missing records, and began to explain that it surely would have been a result of the hospital receiving a request from a lawyer's office for medical records. At this point, I enlightened him what the first week after James's death was like for me. An eleven day old has very few personal effects. James' effects were medical records. The day after I buried him, I hand wrote a request for my son's records on a piece of notepaper.

Silence.

"Are there specific questions you have that I could help you with; understanding that I do not have the files with me?"

To jog his memory, I told him what I knew technically, "You performed open heart surgery with deep hypothermic circulatory arrest to correct a discrete coarctation of the aorta that my son was born with."

"There is a lot for a surgeon and cardiac center director to handle. I would have had an associate perform an echocardiogram to ascertain…"

I interrupted with what I knew already, "Yes, Dr. Bhat performed the echocardiogram."

He agreed, "I would concur with whatever Dr. Bhat said." Well, I knew that very well. I pointed out to him in the same words I used in my deposition, "Dr Bhat had said, 'We are not talking open heart surgery here'."

Again, he said he would agree with whatever Bhat would have advised after the echo.

I explained about the line he drew down his chest and that I was held in court and deposition as conniving or an idiot for not gathering that meant open heart surgery.

He was sticking with me through this and not hanging up. "Well, I cannot remember all aspects of this case without records in front of me," he said. "I would be happy to take a look at them and go over with you everything that is in them and explain it."

Deeper breaths. Careful wording. I went ahead and asked what I felt so strongly about for so long. I was even afraid to ask Jim to ask him. It was so unreal to put it in words. Did you kill James? After just a second of waffling, "The last operation you performed on my son…the one to remove the pinholes in his right lung….."

He interrupted me, "Oh, yes I remember. When a neonate is on a ventilator too long their lungs become…"

It was not necessary for me to hear what I already learned after four years of civil action. I continued, "…another pediatric cardio-thoracic surgeon said he would never have put a child on bypass in that condition to do a lobectomy." I had to stop and just get to the point, "Did you go through re-patching and doing all that so James would not make it home?"

"No. Absolutely not! You're talking about monsters. You are talking about there being monsters walking around." He went on for a minute or two. "How awful for you to walk around all this time thinking that. That has to be something very hard to live with, the belief that such monsters exist."

I felt he was trying to connect with me. Or, he was trying to make me the insane one that could think such a crazy thought to even speak it.

We agreed that this was a hard road for a mother to haul. I assured him I am actually quite all right. He heard of my direction to either go into health care or the law, but then I found a new emerging social science that, done well, could re-engage the trustful physician-patient relationship. One that lawyers did not have to be a part of, yet their presence, as I see it, if handled the way the Beasleys practiced law, would be a benefit to clients, counselors, and physicians. I told him despite being accepted into law school, I turned it down for a couple of reason. One was economics. "Oh, you would be a very good lawyer," he said with seeming sincerity.

The conversation floated into medical malpractice and tort reform issues. "As an individual it is very hard to be a surgeon," Norwood said. "How many lawyers get sued for malpractice?" I was waiting for him to answer but he was actually now waiting for my response.

"I don't know."

"How many mechanics get sued for malpractice?"

"I don't know," I replied wondering if he was actually comparing the high stakes of a two-day-old's entire future to that of a four-year-old Volvo or Hyundai?

"Patients are creating malpractice," he said. "There is no other profession that is subject to the notion of malpractice." As our conversation flowed, there were points we agreed on; specifically, the lack of accountability of the insurance industry. Norwood was pleased to share the statistics with which he was familiar: "There are more medical malpractice cases in Philadelphia than in the entire state of California."

I stated that in Pennsylvania, the number of medical malpractice cases have declined significantly since Act 13 of 2002 had been put in play. Act 13 was Pennsylvania's attempt at tort reforms to reduce medical liability premiums for physicians. It also created the Pennsylvania Patient Safety Authority. This entity is responsible for collecting data on preventable errors. The Patient Safety Authority data showed a large number of preventable errors reported in 2007 despite the decline in medical malpractice cases making it to the civil justice system. After all the drama and tragedy, we were talking shop. I asked him where he was finding his information.

"I get my information from the Society of Thoracic Surgeons."

I was picking my battles. He was talking. "First of all nothing is 100% safe," he said. "How do you define sentinel events? There are things that are being called sentinel that are not and are also not preventable anyway."

These were familiar topics and common ways for them to be argued. I wondered if James was looking down in disappointment for me to be speaking to this man. Maybe he was helping his little brother rest so I could get this conversation in full.

The topic of informed consent arose. Norwood said, "Informed consent is a complete fallacy. It gives parents, patients the feeling of being in charge. That is false. It is a complete fallacy."

How terrifying that one with such power could think this! As he was speaking, I wondered how it was possible that Dr. Nick and Dr. Norwood were admitted to practice surgery. Two such diametrically opposing views and approaches.

I posed a question, "Why is there such a diversity of levels of quality of care in medicine and surgery?" Remembering the multitude of studies on the correlation of medical students' incidents of un-professionalism and the increased likelihood of medical malpractice in their careers," I asked. "Wouldn't it be safer if medical schools were easier to get into, but harder to graduate out of?"

"Bad doctoring stops in a heartbeat," he replied. It's not the schooling.

It is set deep in one's personality."

I was silent, shaking my head. Did I miss something? Who was I talking to?

Norwood suggested an exercise for us. "You tell me how you would have a doctor handle the daily traumas," he said. "You have a doctor who has a patient that is expected to live that then has to go home to his family then is supposed to turn around the next morning and do the same thing with a patient that is just like the one the day before. What would you suggest they do to survive?"

I had an answer but I hesitated. He upped the ante. "You tell me how you would do it, then I will tell you what I do."

On the exhale, "You know Dr. Lown?"

"Who?"

"Dr Bernard Lown, he is a famous cardiologist."

"Well, not that famous, " Norwood admonished. I was shocked. Lown had won the Nobel Peace Prize and identified a means in the mid twentieth century to diagnosis congenital heart defects without invasive means.

I continued in a different direction. "After each shift, as a part of the end of the shift those on the floor, unit, OR should sit in a circle and process with just a sentence or two as to what just happened and how it affected them."

He was quiet. I went on, "This would afford an opportunity as clinicians to understand the anguish and sorrow that might be felt at a loss or unexpected outcome is not a unique experience. It may offer the opportunity for a stronger, healthier camaraderie. It will also serve as an alert to a caregiver who is unprofessional and dangerous to themselves or others. In this circle of community members, they will be more apt to hold each other accountable. Yup, sounds granola."

"That is very close. That is a good suggestion and close to what needs to be done. For me – I'm sort of different. Well, I don' t think I can say. Well, you told me and I did say I would tell you what I do...but.."

He never did say what he does. Or what he did. I inadvertently made it easier for him to step aside that commitment with my own discomfort and awe of how long this discussion had been going on, "You know I don't mean to keep you any more."

Then he offered, "You know none of this is your fault." I was silent as he went on that direction for a bit. There was no apology. There was no admission of guilt or recognition of his accountability in James's death. He seemed to want to relieve me of some guilt.

"I am this child's mother. A mother's job is to see that child through to adulthood. I did not succeed in that. I failed. I am ashamed of my part in that."

"There is absolutely nothing you could have done that would have brought about a different outcome." He repeated, "None of this is your fault."

As a mom, I respectfully, disagreed.

"Well, I said my best."

I didn't say it but I was thinking: If I had just listened to my instincts or walked away or not gone there or not trusted him, my baby would be 7 and we wouldn't be having this conversation. I did remind him of what I had said earlier, "I am actually very good but this is what I would live with. I am not the only mom to live with it."

"You do seem to very well. Very sound of mind."

I was trying to close the conversation. That politeness got in the way and I resisted hanging up on him when he brought up a new topic.

"I was just in Florida to receive an award and there was a colleague there that had something on his mind." He went on but it seemed insignificant to me. It had something to do with the different ways people handle things. This seemed to be about a doctor who had to have a drink either before or after surgery. Or maybe it was both.

Then something connected for Norwood. "Now, I know your son. It is surfacing in my mind." We had just spoken for an hour. I was thrown off center because I was of the impression he already knew of whom he was speaking. I just listened as he spoke, "There is no question that something happened not long after surgery that had to do with ventilator support – which made the heart and lungs unhappy – as a consequence there was a crash."

Yes, I knew this. Thanks to Jim.

Norwood went on, "Then they had to utilize extra-corporeal circulatory support."

Yup, that was the "milkshake machine" that they put him on without any painkillers. Speaking to adults who have lived through anesthesia awareness describe it that it feels like jet-fuel going in you when you receive a paralytic without painkillers. Infants are no more than nerve endings and centers of senses. James received no comforting measures despite being set ablaze from within.

As Norwood went on I looked out the kitchen window to the bright blue afternoon sky and the bird soaring overhead. "There was a problem," he said. "It is like falling down a hill." Jim's "parade of horrible" description was much more accurate to the experience but I continued to listen.

"It's very hard to stop or to get back up. Not everyone can be resuscitated," Norwood declared. "Not everyone can recover," he said.

I wondered to myself who makes that decision. At what point of care are a family's perspectives and opinions sought? I interrupted him, again, expressing what I feel, "I knew about all I would be allowed to know."

He asked why I had released him from the case. Stumbling a bit over my words, I said, "it was the best that we could do at that time. We had to prepare for a jury at that point. I can't completely answer that for you." I didn't want to tell him everything. I had my reasons, and they were mine.

We reviewed again about the missing records. "Every clinician witness that testified said these records would have helped them understand what happened to James," I said.

"You mean every plaintiff's expert!"

"No – I mean both defense and plaintiff's witnesses."

Silence.

He went back to what he believed was the driving force in litigation, "It is all about moving money. Follow the money trail."

I could certainly understand that. Yet, it was terribly ironic that the court could not define my child's worth and yet the bench was paid for his time, as were his staff and aides. The defense counsel had a team show up there everyday for a week. They brought in a window-size blow-up of lab values.

Defense counsel used what sounded a lot like my son's case as a bullet point on his website to drum up more business:

"served as trial counsel in wrongful death action resulting in jury verdict for hospital and physicians in case alleging malpractice for care provided to a newborn immediately following cardiac surgery."

Norwood, the doctors, the nurses, the hospital executives and their risk managers were all paid for the time.

The jury all lost their regular week's pay from their jobs for about $9 a day. So, how much was James worth?

Norwood stated, "Litigation is no way to solve complicated scientific problems."

I shared with Norwood the verdict. He was insensed, "That is a non-sequitor. That is a complete non-sequitor for me. That just doesn't make any sense." He wanted me to explain it. He wasn't sure whether to believe me. There was nothing for me to say. He had taken the words right out of Jim's mouth. On this, we would all agree.

The doctor repeatedly said for me to send him a copy of the book when finished with an invoice. He would love a copy. "I would pay for that absolutely," he said.

I was left feeling he wanted to hear from me again. More importantly, I left the conversation not needing anything more.

He was still the same as he had been in deposition. He was the same as he had been when avoiding me as the mother of a patient of his that he had injured. He really hadn't changed. I didn't feel any new sense of compassion. He seemed only compassionate to his own purposes; which is why it was easy for us to exchange thoughts on medical malpractice litigation. My goal is to ease it for patients and physicians and he falls into that beneficiary group. It's a money trail of sorts. Speaking to me worked for him now. There is no threat from me seven years after the wrongful death. All civil litigation was exhausted.

I had not fully prepared myself for the phone call by creating a list of questions. There was no premeditated strategy. All I knew was I had to offer an opportunity for him to address the issues this book discussed. It was a shock that he was so open to talking to me. Yet, he did. I am grateful to him for that. Though I still wish I had never met him, or Jim for that matter, I appreciate that in all the pain and sadness at some point this surgeon was willing to still try to help me understand.

It took years through litigation, trial, grief and living to bring us together again. We may not agree on everything. The effect of the events on each of us are different. But, we did seem to agree that there should have been more communication and opportunity to understand long before my call. It would have saved all the professionals and lay people involved millions of dollars. It would have offered the opportunity of saving the life of another baby.

I no longer see the stars, I am the stars.

I no longer breathe the wind; I am the wind.

I am the sweet smell of honeysuckle after an

Evening rain.

I am the dew on the rose petals in early

morning.

I am harmony and I am peace.

I am love.

In sorrow, my mother and father cry, but

they need not fear.

For I am strong, my heart is whole and in

union with my soul.

I understand my fate, and I smile

For nature's will is my destiny and my guide

through eternity.

~ Michael Berman, MD

Resources

Learn more about improving doctor-patient communication, improving pediatric patient safety and how you can help at www.jamessproject.com.

If you are a patient, family member, or health care provider suffering complex grief or stress from iatrogenic injury consider reaching out to one of the following organizations.

Compassion in Healthcare – www.compassioninhealthcare.org

Consumers Advancing Patient Safety – www.caps.org

Medically Induced Trauma Support Service – www.MITSS.org

The Empowered Patient Coalition – www.TheEmpoweredPatient.com

Voice for Patients – www.voice4patients.com

References

Braithwaite, J. 1989. *Crime, shame, and reintegration.* New York : Cambridge, MA. University Press. (Chapters 1 and 4-7).

Christie, N. (1977). Conflict as property. *The British Journal of Criminology*, 1-14.

Crane, M. (2008, April 4). Doctors who became lawyers: what they want you to know. Medical economics.

Corrigan, J., Kohn, L., 1997. To err is human: building a safer health care system. Committee on quality of health care in America , Institute of medicine. Washington , DC .

Gibson, Rosemary (2003). The wall of silence: the untold story of the medical mistakes that kill and injure millions of Americans. Lifeline Press.

Kim, W. & Mauborgne, R. (1997). Fair process: Managing in the knowledge economy. Harvard Business Review, 75(4), 65-75.

Lown, Bernard, MD. 1996. *The lost art of healing.* Ballantine Books.

References

Mannix v. Nemours et al, 2005. Superior Court of Delaware, Wilmington , DE .

Mannix v. Nemours, et al, April 11, 2006, Delaware State Superior Court transcripts.

Nuland, Sherwin B., The Doctors' Plague, W.W. Norton & Co., 2003.

Palmer, P. 1998. The courage to teach. Jossey-Bass Inc. San Francisco, CA

Wachtel, T. 1997. *Real justice*. The Piper's Press, Pipersville, PA.

Wallace B., Damages, Philadelphia Magazine, September 2001

Weingarten, K. (2003). *Common Shock*. New York : Dutton Books.